Writing Your Life

Fourth Edition

Writing Your Life

A Guide to Writing Autobiographies

Mary Borg

Illustrated by Joyce Turley

PRUFROCK PRESS INC.
WACO, TEXAS

To my mother, my three sisters,
my husband, and my five sons,
with thanks for their encouragement and love,
and, for this last edition, to
my 10 grandchildren, who
have added tremendous joy to my life.

Library of Congress Cataloging-in-Publication Data

Borg, Mary.
Writing Your Life : A Guide to Writing Autobiographies / By Mary Borg ; Illustrated by Joyce Turley.
   pages cm
Originally published by: Fort Collins, Colorado : Cottonwood Press under the title Writing your life
: an easy-to-follow guide to writing an autobiography, 1998.
   ISBN 978-1-61821-026-5 (pbk.)
1. Autobiography--Authorship. 2. Report writing. I. Turley, Joyce Mihran, illustrator. II. Title.
CT25.B67 2013
808.06'692--dc23
                              2012040615

The author gratefully acknowledges the use of the following copyrighted material: "Milkmen Lost in Generation Gap," by Guernsey Le Pelley. Copyright © 1987. Reprinted by permission of Guernsey Le Pelley.

Edited by Sean Redmond

Cover and layout design by Raquel Trevino

Illustrations by Joyce Turley

ISBN-13: 978-1-61821-026-5

Printed in the United States of America.

Prufrock Press Inc.
P.O. Box 8813
Waco, TX 76714-8813
Phone: (800) 998-2208
Fax: (800) 240-0333
http://www.prufrock.com

Table of Contents

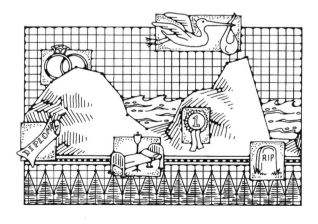

Acknowledgments

I am grateful to the many senior adults who have enrolled in my *Writing Your Life* classes over the years. They have helped me to become, not just a better teacher, but also a better person. They have taught me much about life and love—and about aging with humor, joy, integrity, patience and enthusiasm.

I am grateful to Susan Malmstadt, former director of senior education at Aims Community College, for her enthusiastic endorsement of the idea for this book.

I am grateful to Dawn DiPrince, the production manager for the previous edition of *Writing Your Life*, for her exceptional organization skills.

I am grateful to Sean Redmond, the very capable editor of this new edition of *Writing Your Life*, for his encouragement and forthrightness.

I am grateful to the editor and publisher of the first edition of this book, Cheryl Miller Thurston, for her patience, good cheer, invaluable knowledge, hard work, amazing editing skills, and friendship during the writing of the book, for without her, this book would not be.

I would also like to thank the following men and women for use of their autobiographical materials:

- Benita Ackerman
- Carroll Arnold, *Nothin's Easy*
- Iva Bjorneby
- Bernie Bliss, *Roots, Blossoms, Wings*
- Mary Casseday, *Pathways*
- Hazel Chick, *Memory Is the Haunting of the Heart*
- Paul W. Clancy, *Well, I Thought It Was Interesting*

- Agnes Clausen, *The Track of the Wooden Shoes*
- Marge Curtiss
- Donna Davis, *Dancing in the Cactus Patch*
- Norma Erickson, *Coming to a New Land*
- Clare Foster, *Roses and Thorns*
- Marie Giesler, *Sentimental Journey*
- Julia L. "Judy" Graham, *My Life*
- Barbara Anne Green, *Journals*
- Myrt Grooms, *The Unraveling*
- Peggy Hess, *Bits and Pieces of My Life*
- Marietta Hetherington Neumeister
- Ron Hildebrand, *Might as Well, Can't Dance*
- Sally Howard, *Work in Progress*
- Mary Irwin, *Who's Got the Toothbrush?*
- Bob Jackson
- Ivan Klein, *The Autobiography of Ivan Klein*
- Mary Koenig, *My Story*
- Bernie Lynch
- Bernie Malnati, *Is That the Truth, Mom, or Did You Make It Up?*
- Delia Grubb Martin, *Yesterday*
- Joseph Wilson Mefford, Jr., *My Story, My Song*
- John Mills
- Joan Milne, *And So It Was*
- Marietta Hetherington Neumeister
- Lois Osborn, *Eight Decades*
- Charles A. Phillips, *Dryland Diary*
- Lorene Putnam
- Eldon Risser, *The Years of My Life*
- Orren Gilbert Scholfield, *Many Cherries, Some Pits*
- Sue Schulze, *No Fun Like Work*
- Mary Skuderna
- Viola Smith, *Here I Am*
- Dean Sommers
- Uba Stanley, *Uba Stanley's Sojourn on This Planet Earth*
- Wally Stewart
- Helen Tisdel
- Robert Vail, *Dew on a Leaf*
- Cleo Wadleigh
- Janet Williamson, *My Story*
- Fred Wurtsmith, *It's Been a Long Road*
- Helene Yurman, *Who Am I?*
- Mark Yurman, *My Biography*

Mary Borg

Introduction

THE STORY OF
WRITING YOUR LIFE

It all started because of Ethel. Ethel was one of my students in a class called "Twentieth Century American Leaders and How They Changed Our Lives." One day, as the senior adults in the class were talking about the past, Ethel got a sad, wistful look on her face. "How I wish I had written down or tape-recorded my father's stories," she said.

Heads nodded around the table. Everyone knew what she meant. They all wished they had done the same thing. Soon they were talking about their own stories. Shouldn't they be writing them down for their own children and grandchildren?

Before I knew it, I had volunteered to teach a class, agreeing to help them remember and write about their lives. Everyone got excited—everyone except one rosy-cheeked woman named Nettie, who said, "I worked for the telephone company for 34 years, and nothing exciting ever happened to me. I wouldn't have anything to write." Still, she agreed to try.

I decided the first assignment should be about ancestors. I made up a list of questions for students to answer, just to get them started, and sent them off to write. The next week, somewhat apprehensively, I met the group again. Had the assignment been too lengthy, too vague, too hard? What if all that initial enthusiasm had waned? What if no one had written a word?

Very shyly, Nettie, the telephone operator, volunteered to read what she had written. Her story included an entire history of the migration of Western Europeans to Russia during the latter half of the 18th century. She wrote about the opportunities offered by the Russian czarina Catherine the Great, who gave free land to settlers. She wrote about the Russian military draft at the turn of the century, immigration to the United States, and the settling of the West under the U.S. Homestead Act. It was a beautifully written story, and she had not referred to any history book. She had simply written what she had learned from listening to her mother's stories. And she had thought she wouldn't have anything to write!

Martha, a woman with no formal education past the eighth grade, offered to read next. She read about her mother, whose husband had died and left her with four small children to raise alone. As Martha read, I could see her mother, a strong pioneer woman who showed her children the small joys of life: picnics, good food, sharing with neighbors. Fun and love were precious gifts, and selfishness, pettiness, and prejudice had no place in her world. Martha's eyes misted, her voice quavered, and all of us were deeply touched. In our hearts, we hoped that our sons and daughters could someday write with the same love about us, and that we would leave them with such lovely memories.

The students were hooked. Week after week, I came up with questions and activities to guide them. Week after week, they shared their stories.

Lydia wrote about her father, who was lured to the California grape country before World War I, thinking to make big money. Then one day he came home and announced, "We're going back to Colorado. In Colorado you can brush the snow off your shoulders, but in California the rain seeps through your clothes, and you never get warm."

Doris wrote about the day, at age 12, that she ran after her father with the sack lunch he had left on the kitchen table. She ran several blocks, calling his name, and finally caught up to him. He thanked her and said he could have gotten along without it that day, that she needn't have run so far. And then, with tears in her eyes, Doris read the simple words, "He never ate his lunch that day. He had a heart attack and died at age 48."

Ethel wrote about the childhood summer she and her mother and siblings spent in quarantine because of an illness. Gladys wrote about how she and her 12 brothers and sisters were farmed out to relatives and foster homes after her mother died. Clyde wrote about Halloween pranks: pushing over outhouses, stomping watermelons, putting a man's new wagon up on top of the schoolhouse. Sophie wrote about meeting her husband-to-be, Shorty, on a blind date. Pauline wrote about plowing through Montana winters and about sneaking over to the Native American burial grounds to find bones and relics of the Sioux.

All of this took place 23 years ago. Since that first, hesitant beginning, the autobiography group has grown into a series of three, college quarter-length classes. Scores of men and women have completed autobiographies, had them "published," and given them to relatives, to rave reviews. Hundreds of others have never finished a book, but they have written stories: lots of stories. Even in first-draft form, the stores are sure to be cherished by future generations. Dozens of other men and women are still actively writing, aiming to finish their autobiographies in the next year or two.

In 1989, I gathered together all of the materials I had used with my students over the years and, with the help of my then-editor, Cheryl Miller Thurston, put them into one easy-to-use manual. The book was designed to help anyone write an autobiography, whether writing alone or with the support of an informal group of friends or an organized class. Now the book is being used in Writing Your Life classes all over the country: in hospitals, community colleges, senior centers, nursing homes, recreation centers—wherever people recognize the importance of recording life stories.

And now I have updated the book, making it—I hope—even more flexible, easy-to-use, and appropriate for adults writing in the 21st century.

I hope you enjoy the book. More importantly, I hope you enjoy the journey you are about to take—a journey back through the memories of your life. Good luck!

WELCOME TO WRITING YOUR LIFE

Writing an autobiography is a big task. In order to make that task more manageable, *Writing Your Life* is divided into five chapters.

CHAPTER 1: A FEW BASICS

This section points out some of the rewards of writing an autobiography, provides reasons for why people write them, and gives practical tips about getting started.

CHAPTER 2: LAYING THE GROUNDWORK

This section offers information on genealogy and tips on conducting genealogical research. It also includes a chapter on technology and explains how computer software and websites can assist you with your writing.

CHAPTERS 3 AND 4: REMEMBERING AND WRITING, EARLY YEARS AND ADULT YEARS

These two chapters make up the largest portion of *Writing Your Life* and include several kinds of material:

➼ **Questions to Explore.** These lists of questions are designed to stimulate your memory. You can answer all of the questions or only the ones that appeal to you, and you can answer them in any order or lack thereof. Remember: The word *author* is the base of the word of the word *authority*. There is no recipe for writing an autobiography; these questions are merely reminders and suggestions.

•❖ **Writing Tips.** Writing tips are also included in these chapters. Although the purpose of *Writing Your Life* is not to teach you how to write, the writing tips do provide valuable advice.

•❖ **Reading Suggestions.** Reading suggestions relate to the topic of each subsection. Materials are recommended for both inspiration and enjoyment.

•❖ **In the Words of Real People.** Selections from the writings of ordinary men and women are included throughout *Writing Your Life*. They are taken from autobiographical pieces of *Writing Your Life* students and others.

Informational materials are also provided throughout the book, as are quotations, included for both amusement and contemplation.

CHAPTER 5: PUTTING IT ALL TOGETHER

This section gives practical information about putting your book together and "publishing" it for family and friends.

APPENDIX: DECADES

This section offers historical topics, trends, and events by decade that can be helpful when writing your autobiography.

Chapter 1
A Few Basics

"The longer I live the more beautiful life becomes." —Frank Lloyd Wright

JOIN A LONG LINE OF AUTOBIOGRAPHY WRITERS

Since the dawn of consciousness, people have felt compelled to share their lives with future generations. As you write about your memories, you join a long line of autobiography writers.

All writers have different motives, but most people write their autobiographies for some combination of the reasons listed below. Perhaps some of these reasons will be your reasons.

To set the record straight. Out of the Watergate affair, for instance, almost every major player wrote a book. Some examples:

- *Blind Ambition: The White House Years* by John Dean

- *The Whole Truth: The Watergate Conspiracy* by Sam J. Ervin, Jr.

To instruct, so that others may learn from their lives. Some examples:

- *An Autobiography: The Story of My Experiments With Truth* by Mohandas Gandhi

- *Having Our Say: The Delany Sisters' First 100 Years* by Sarah and A. Elizabeth Delany

- *The Autobiography of Benjamin Franklin* by Benjamin Franklin

To explain how they overcame handicaps and adversity, as a testimony to achievement against all odds. Some examples:

- *The Story of My Life* by Helen Keller

- *Up From Slavery* by Booker T. Washington

- *I Know Why the Caged Bird Sings* by Maya Angelou

- *Lucky Man: A Memoir* by Michael J. Fox

- *The Woman I Was Born to Be: My Story* by Susan Boyle

To act as historians of major events in which they participated. Some examples:

- *Memoirs of the Second World War* by Winston Churchill

- *Madam Secretary: A Memoir* by Madeleine Albright

To leave a legacy. Many individuals want to share their lives with their descendants, or to tell future generations about their world. Some examples:

- *Growing Up* by Russell Baker

- *An American Childhood* by Annie Dillard

- *The Life and Times of the Thunderbolt Kid: A Memoir* by Bill Bryson

To keep busy. Sometimes people write because they need something interesting and productive to do with their time. Some examples:

- *The Diary of a Young Girl* by Anne Frank
- *The Year of Magical Thinking* by Joan Didion

To tell about a memorable experience. Some examples:

- *We: The Daring Flyer's Remarkable Life Story and His Account of the Transatlantic Flight That Shook the World* by Charles Lindbergh
- *The Blue Jay's Dance: A Memoir of Early Childhood* by Louise Erdrich
- *The Last True Story I'll Ever Tell: An Accidental Soldier's Account of the War in Iraq* by John Crawford
- *Bird Cloud: A Memoir of Place* by Annie Proulx

To share. Some people write about their lives simply because they want to or because they believe others will be interested. Some examples:

- *My Lucky Stars: A Hollywood Memoir* by Shirley MacLaine
- *All Creatures Great and Small* by James Herriot
- *One Writer's Beginnings* by Eudora Welty
- *An Hour Before Daylight: Memories of a Rural Boyhood* by Jimmy Carter
- *Living to Tell the Tale* by Gabriel García Márquez
- *Eat, Pray, Love* by Elizabeth Gilbert

To boost their stature in the political arena. Some examples:

- *Living History* by Hillary Rodham Clinton
- *Dreams From My Father: A Story of Race and Inheritance* by Barack Obama
- *No Apology: The Case for American Greatness* by Mitt Romney
- *Going Rogue: An American Life* by Sarah Palin

To try to understand the past or to make sense of life. Some examples:

- *Angela's Ashes: A Memoir* by Frank McCourt
- *Blindsided: Lifting a Life Above Illness: A Reluctant Memoir* by Richard M. Cohen
- *Slaves in the Family* by Edward Ball
- *The Glass Castle: A Memoir* by Jeannette Walls

THE REWARDS OF WRITING AN AUTOBIOGRAPHY

People who have used *Writing Your Life* report that writing their life stories is an incredibly rewarding experience. Even those who never quite complete the project say the writing experience has been a highlight of their later years. Here are just a few of the rewards men and women have reported:

- *Satisfaction.* There is satisfaction and pride involved in writing a book. Writing an autobiography is not easy, and individuals who finish feel justifiably proud. Again and again, writers tell of feeling an enormous sense of satisfaction upon completing their stories.

- *The joy of giving.* Finishing an autobiography allows writers the joy of giving a truly special, one-of-a-kind gift. Writers are often delighted by the positive responses they receive from their children, grandchildren, and even great-grandchildren.

  Many writers give their finished books to relatives as Christmas gifts. One married couple wrote their stories individually, had them bound together, and gave the finished book to their children at the couple's 50th wedding anniversary party.

  Whatever the occasion, the gift of a loved one's autobiography is a special gift indeed.

➤ *Healing.* No matter how old we are—17 or 77—we are all searching for identity, meaning, and purpose in our lives. Often, in the process of recording their lives, writers find that old wounds heal, misunderstandings clear up, irritations with others disappear, and the pain of a secret hurt fades. Again and again, writers tell of the peace and understanding that comes from writing their memoirs.

One mother wrote of nursing her son through a year of pain after he suffered first degree burns on three-quarters of his 7-year-old body. For the first time, the woman saw the strength it had taken for both her and her son to survive. Another woman wrote about being sexually abused by her brother when she was very young—and about her confused feelings as she continued to love him, although hating what he had done to her, even after his death. Through writing the story, she at last found peace.

One man wrote about looking forward to his retirement years, only to discover he must spend his days caring for a wife with a debilitating disease. He shared his anger and frustration, receiving sympathy from other *Writing Your Life* classmates who shared tales of similar experiences. The support of other writers helped him to face the terrible difficulties he must contend with each day.

➤ *Self-discovery.* People who write about their lives also learn about themselves. They discover that they are survivors. They discover that they have achieved some measure of success in their lives—whether mentally, socially, physically, emotionally and/or spiritually. They realize that they have led the only life they could have led. They accept their choices. They discover themselves.

GETTING STARTED

Writing your life story will be easier if you make a date with your memories. In other words, set aside a certain time each week for writing. Then discipline yourself to stick to your schedule.

For example, you might decide that every Tuesday morning, from 9:00 to noon, you will write—without fail. Have everything ready before you begin: a certain kind of pen, background music, your laptop, a cup of coffee, whatever makes you feel most comfortable.

Before the date with yourself each week, review the questions you will be working on. Let them "simmer" on the back burner of your mind. Then, when you sit down to write, you will be surprised at all of the work your mind will already have done.

Whatever you do, don't wait for inspiration to hit. It probably won't. If you force yourself to sit down and write something, you will be surprised at how easy it is to continue. The actual act of writing is the best stimulus for thoughts and ideas.

BE PRACTICAL

Use a three-ring notebook for your writing, and insert your handwritten or typed pages. You will often find yourself wanting to go back and add paragraphs or even whole pages to your work. With a three-ring notebook, it is easy to insert materials, and you can also use the backs of the pages you have already written. If you use a spiral notebook, it will be harder to add to your writing and harder to keep your material organized.

USE A COMPUTER

If you have access to a computer, this is a great time to use it—or learn to use it. Writing is so much easier with a computer, and it is easy to learn the basics of most word processing programs. Many colleges and recreation programs offer computer classes, and if you really find yourself struggling, it should be easy to find an individual to help you—perhaps a friend, a family member, or a hired tutor.

One *Writing Your Life* student had this to say on the subject of computers:

> Fortunately I have a word processing program. The facility with which editing, deleting, or adding can be made gives me the patience to continue. I could not have done it on a typewriter . . . partially because I cannot touch-type and consequently make many typos.
>
> I still fumble at the keys and have to search the keyboard for every letter, but at the end of every sentence or paragraph, I can run my cursor back on the screen and make any necessary corrections.
>
> Such lack of typing skill is not very conducive to creative writing, as the mind outpaces the dreary mechanical functions. My solution to this, oddly enough, is to put my ideas down on yellow legal pads in longhand and later transcribe them to the computer's memory and printer.
>
> Mark Yurman, *My Biography*

Technology does have its drawbacks, however. One *Writing Your Life* author, long ago, bought a word-processing typewriter to help him with his autobiography. However, the spell checker on the machine didn't recognize "y'all" as a legitimate word. Every time the Southern gentleman typed "y'all"—which was frequently—the machine beeped. The man became so annoyed that he finally packed up the machine, returned it, and went back to his ancient and sensible old typewriter, a typewriter that had no objection to a fine old Southern word like "y'all."

A computer today won't beep at you if you spell out words it doesn't like, but programs like Microsoft Word will typically underline unrecognized entries in red. If you find this feature bothersome, however, you can turn it off.

USE "QUESTIONS TO EXPLORE" AS MEMORY JOGGERS

The Questions to Explore are meant to be used as memory joggers, as guidelines, as possibilities. Not every question will be appropriate for every person. In answering the questions, let your writing flow from topic to topic. Don't pause and write, "In answer to question 4, I remember my mother always making us swallow a tablespoon of cod liver oil each morning." Use each set of questions as memory aids, not as an assignment that must be completed item by item, as if you were back in junior high.

A helpful technique is to take notes as you read a new set of questions. Beside each question, jot down specific incidents or people to write about as they come to mind. Then you can refer back to your notes as you write.

BELIEVE IN YOURSELF

No one else can write the story you are about to write. If you don't, no one will. (Or worse: someone will, and they will get it wrong!) Believe in yourself. After all, you are the expert on the topic you will be writing about—your own life.

STAYING MOTIVATED

Although writing an autobiography is a rewarding activity, it is not always easy. It is sometimes hard to stay motivated, to discipline yourself, and to keep going.

Many people work best in a group setting, where they are poked and prodded into action and feel obligated to come prepared. If you are a person who needs a bit of structure to stay motivated, try one of the following suggestions:

- ❧ Organize an informal writing group with a few friends. Meet weekly to share your writing and to give each other support and encouragement.

- Ask a local community college, church, or senior center to organize a Writing Your Life class. A class setting has a number of benefits. It is easier to keep working because you have assignments to complete each week. It is easier to stay motivated because you have a weekly audience to listen to what you have written and to give you support and encouragement. Listening to other people's stories can jog your memory and help you write. Sharing with others in a class is also a good way to solve any problems you encounter.

- Start and lead your own Writing Your Life class. Put an invitation on the bulletin board of your church, apartment building, or senior citizen center noting the date, time, and place of the first meeting. You might want to charge a small fee to cover any costs you anticipate, such as room rental, advertising, or refreshments, and ask each student to get a copy of *Writing Your Life* in advance. You won't really have to teach, just act as a group leader or facilitator and make the sharing of writing the focus of class.

- Set up a "correspondence course" with a distant sibling. Promise each other to write a chapter a week, and then exchange copies through e-mail or regular mail. Before you start, talk about the importance of being accepting and positive. Brothers and sisters often remember events in different ways, but that is because they have different perspectives. It is important not to criticize each other's work—just to share.

- You know yourself well. If you know you need structure, find it. If you know you work well on your own, carry on. Either way, enjoy yourself.

YOU CAN DO IT!

When it comes to writing, many people suffer from a lack of self-confidence. "I don't have anything to write about," they say. "I've never done anything especially interesting or been anywhere exciting. My life has been just a life, nothing special."

They are wrong. Every life is special. Every life is worth writing about.

Are you one of those people reluctant to begin your memoirs? Here are a few things to think about:

- ●◆ Consider the dramatic changes you have seen in your life. Those changes range from technological advances in food preparation, transportation, medicine, and communication to changes in family life, the roles of husbands and wives, and the attitudes and expectations of our society. You are an expert on change; you have survived.

  Even if you were to write about nothing but change, you would have more than enough material for a book that would fascinate your descendants.

- ●◆ Think about what you remember most from autobiographies you have read or stories you have heard about famous people. Most of us do not remember much about the historical events, public successes, or political decisions that make people famous. It is the human stories that we remember most. For example, I don't remember the wording of the Gulf of Tonkin Resolution of 1964, which gave President Johnson the power to wage war in Southeast Asia, or of the Great Society speech he gave at the University of Michigan—but I certainly remember when he showed his gallbladder operation stitches to the world!

  Older generations may not remember the details of the Berlin airlift or the Fair Deal of Harry S. Truman. But if they are like most people of that era, they remember more clearly the letter Truman wrote to the music critic of the *Washington Post*, a critic who had roasted a singing recital by Truman's daughter. Truman wrote, "You sound like a frustrated old man who never made a success . . . I never met you, but if I do you'll need a new nose and a supporter below." People remember that story because it is human—a feisty man losing his temper and rushing to the defense of his daughter. That is something we can relate to.

All lives are filled with stories. All men and women have stories to tell—funny, interesting, embarrassing, painful, delightful, sad, or whimsical stories about themselves, the people they have known, and the people they have loved. You may not be able to recall your stories easily, but they are there. *Writing Your Life* is designed to help you remember them.

➤ Think about how it would feel to have an autobiography written by one of your parents or grandparents. Wouldn't it be one of your most valued possessions? Most people would treasure the memoirs of one of their ancestors, no matter how "ordinary" that ancestor's life had been. Your descendants are sure to feel the same way.

➤ If you are like most people, you may suffer from a lack of self-confidence about the actual act of writing. Stringing words into well-written, grammatically correct, perfectly punctuated sentences and paragraphs may have you terrified. If so, you are not alone.

Give this idea a try: Plan to write a really terrible first draft. Then do it. Don't worry about details like perfect punctuation and spelling. Just write as much as you can as freely as you can. Editing and rewriting can come later. (You may be surprised when your really terrible first draft turns out to not be terrible at all.) Just think of the things you know and the stories you hold in your heart. You can write about soda jerks, dust bowl storms, victory gardens, Rosie the Riveter, Edward R. Murrow, kick the can, party lines, wringer washers, Elvis, Woodstock, Norman Rockwell covers of the *Saturday Evening Post*, Johnny Carson, the *Challenger* explosion, the end of the Cold War, the Clinton impeachment trials, Y2K, or September 11th. Everything is worthy of a story.

No matter who you are, you have a lot to tell. You can write your autobiography. It will be fun. It will be rewarding. It will bring you so much pleasure.

Go ahead and start writing. You can do it!

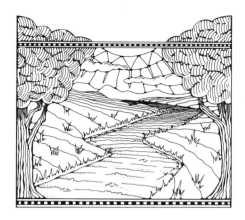

Chapter 2
Laying the Groundwork

"Family means no one gets left behind or forgotten." —David Ogden Stiers

FINDING OUT ABOUT ANCESTORS

Many people beginning their autobiographies are surprised by how little they actually know about their ancestors. They get caught up in the genealogical puzzle of hunting for names and dates. More importantly, they look for information to help flesh out their ancestors and make them real.

If you are interested in your genealogy, there are a number of places that can help you track down your ancestors. Most cities have genealogical society chapters, and chapter volunteers will provide you with tips on how to trace family trees. In many cities the chapters also have reserved sections in local libraries.

The following are some notable organizations that can help you in your search:

- *Family History Library* (http://familysearch.org)—The Family History Library in Salt Lake City, UT, offers the largest collection of genealogical records in the world. There is no charge to look through the archives yourself or you can hire a trained, accredited genealogist there to locate material for you.

  The Church of Jesus Christ of Latter-day Saints operates FamilySearch Centers all over the United States. You can call or write to the address below for a list of centers in your area, or consult the website. Its archives are open to the public. They contain census records, courthouse records, and information about births, deaths, and marriages. More than 3 billion deceased individuals are referenced in their materials. For more information, contact the Church of Jesus Christ of Latter-day Saints, 35 NW Temple Street, Salt Lake City, UT 84103. Phone: 801-240-2584 or 1-866-406-1830.

- *National Genealogical Society* (http://www.ngsgenealogy.org)—This non-profit organization provides educational programs and networking opportunities and publishes the *National Genealogical Society Quarterly* and *NGS Magazine*. The National Genealogical Society is located at 3108 Columbia Pike, Suite 300, Arlington, VA 22204-4370. Phone: 703-525-0050 or 1-800-473-0060.

- *The National Archives and Records Administration* (http://www.archives.gov)—The National Archives contain federal records on microfilm, including records about the census, military service, pensions, citizenship, homestead deeds, and passenger lists. Citizens are granted 72 years of privacy, so documents dating to 1940 and earlier are available. Its address is 700 Pennsylvania Avenue NW, Washington, DC 20408; its mailing address is 8601 Adelphi Road, College Park, MD 20740-6001. Phone: 866-272-6272.

Since the advent of the Internet, genealogical research has become easier than ever. You can find a number of websites that provide information, addresses, and phone numbers for genealogical organizations. Many have a special focus, such as African-American genealogy or Jewish genealogy. To find information that may be helpful to you, simply use a search engine and type in the word *genealogy*, or you can check out some of these popular genealogy websites:

- *Ancestry.com* (http://www.ancestry.com)—This website provides links to many U.S. public records, including census data, military records, and the Social Security Death Index.

- *Genealogy.com* (http://www.genealogy.com)—This website allows a free trial membership for accessing its collection of resources, including family trees and historical records.

- *Library and Archives Canada* (http://bac-lac-.gc.ca/eng/Pages/home.aspx)—This website provides links to Canadian archives.

- *Library of Congress* (http://www.loc.gov)—The Library of Congress' website offers historical newspapers, prints, photographs, documents, veterans' histories, and even early sound recordings.

- *RootsWeb* (http://www.rootsweb.ancestry.com)—This affiliate of Ancestry.com offers resources to help facilitate genealogical research, including mailing lists, message boards, and databases.

- *The National Archives* (http://www.nationalarchives.gov.uk)—This website provides access to the United Kingdom's government records.

- *The WorldGenWeb Project* (http://www.worldgenweb.org)—The WorldGenWeb Project provides free research guidance from a worldwide network of volunteer genealogists.

Many websites also offer further services that you can purchase to help you organize your research into various charts and graphs and give you broader access to genealogical resources.

USING TECHNOLOGY

As technology has advanced, writing your life has, in some ways, become easier than ever. The Internet alone is a powerful tool that can aid you in completing your project. Besides assisting with genealogical research, websites exist that provide detailed information about every major event that's happened throughout history. These websites can spur your memory and help you put your life into a wider historical context. A good place to start is with the popular online encyclopedia Wikipedia, which can be accessed at http://www.wikipedia.com.

Some websites provide rundowns of major events that have taken place on each day of the year. Some examples include:

- *This Day in History* (http://www.history.com/this-day-in-history)

- *On This Day* (http://learning.blogs.nytimes.com/on-this-day)

- *Today in History* (http://www.historynet.com/today-in-history)

And of course, search engines like Google and Yahoo! can help you search for specific information based on keywords that you enter, so if you're trying to remember the name of a place or an event, you can just type in what you know and see what comes up. You never know what you may find—or how what you find may help you remember!

APPS

Application software programs, or *apps*, are staples of computer technology. The term essentially refers to any computer program that can help you perform an activity. If you've used a computer, you've probably used many apps without even realizing it. Recently, the term "app" has grown especially popular in reference to programs for smartphones and tablet computers. Specialized apps for these devices exist that offer all sorts of services, including help with journaling and autobiographical writing. Examples of such apps include Day One (http://dayoneapp.com) and Momento (http://www.momentoapp.com). Each offers unique features to help you get into the habit of writing regularly. You can use them simply as tools to help keep track of your thoughts, or you can create an entire digital record of your life, with detailed entries, photos, and even location and weather information. They are particularly useful for jotting down ideas while on the go. It should be noted, however, that such programs are designed more to help chronicle your life going forward, rather than to help recapture your past.

For an example of how app software has the potential to redefine the limits of traditional autobiography, readers may want to check out I Am Zlatan (http://iamzlatan.com). This interactive autobiography app of soccer star Zlatan Ibrahimović demonstrates some of the ways that app software has expanded the possibilities of what can be achieved in an autobiography.

OTHER WAYS TECHNOLOGY CAN HELP

For those looking to stick with brick and mortar, paper and ink-type products, there are still many technological programs that can assist you in your goal. Helpful tips can be found in Chapter 5 of this book (Putting It All Together). Here, you'll find information on how to use word processing programs like Microsoft Word to strengthen your finished product. You can play with text size, font style, add pictures, and perform all sorts of other design changes with even the most basic programs. You can also do things like add footnotes at the bottom of your pages, to provide explanations of older terms that your grandchildren and other younger readers may not be familiar with. Of course, you have to finish writing your autobiography before you can start worrying about presentation, so now is a good time to continue onto Chapter 3 and begin the journey of *Writing Your Life*!

Chapter 3

Remembering and Writing: Early Years

"I think of life as a good book. The further you get into it, the more it begins to make sense." —Harold S. Kushner

ABOUT YOUR FAMILY

"We all come from the past, and children ought to know what it was that went into their making." —Russell Baker

As you begin writing about your life, don't "get yourself born" yet. Instead, set the scene for your arrival, telling what you know about your family and your ancestors. Go back as far as you can and try to lay down as much detail as possible about the people, the places, and the things that helped shape your entry into the world.

Think of yourself as a playwright. You are setting the stage for your grand arrival. Everyone—your parents and grandparents, aunts and uncles, and older siblings if you have any—are all waiting for *you* to be born! So, just like a playwright, you need to list the main characters the reader will be introduced to and set the scene of the main action before you show up on the stage of your life.

- From what country or countries did your ancestors emigrate? Why did they come to America? How? When? Where did they settle?

- What do you remember most about your mother from your childhood? What was she like? What did she look like? What did you learn from her?

- What do you remember most about your father from your childhood? What was he like? What did he look like? What did you learn from him?

- Tell as much as you can about your grandparents and great-grandparents. Who were they? What were they like?

- What stories have been handed down from generation to generation in your family? Are there any stories known by only a few, stories that are kept secret?

- What values and beliefs were important to your parents? How do you know they were important?

- Who came before you in your family? If you have older brothers and sisters, tell about them. When were they born? How much older are they than you?

- What kind of family did you live in? Describe your family's personality and how it affected you.

- Where did your family live when you were born? Was it on a farm, in a small town, or in a city? Describe the physical setting.

Some say America is made up of three distinct groups: those who were already here, those who were forced to come, and those who chose to come. Those already here were, of course, the members of various Native American tribes. Those forced to come included Irish indentured servants, African slaves, debtors from British prisons, and Chinese railroad workers. Those who chose to come included people who wanted to experience political freedom, economic opportunity, and/or religious tolerance. Many others came to avoid conscription into the armies of various kings, emperors, and czars. Some have said, therefore, that America is really a nation of draft dodgers!

Research the lives of your ancestors and find out under what circumstances they came to America. If you can't find any information, use your imagination and try to picture what your great-great relatives were like as a warm-up to get your cogs of creativity turning.

WRITING TIPS

Be yourself. Write as you talk, and let your personality shine through. Don't worry about grammar, spelling, or organization; just let your words flow. Later you can proofread and edit, or have someone else do it. Finally—and most importantly—tell the truth. Good writing is always honest.

READING SUGGESTIONS

➻ "Aunt Sue's Stories," from *Selected Poems of Langston Hughes* by Langston Hughes—This poem describes the wonder and value of telling real-life stories to a young child. It is a compelling invitation to start writing your stories.

FAMILY TREE

"To move freely, you must be deeply rooted." —*Bella Lewitzky*

Make a family tree to go with your life story. Be sure to include as much information as possible, including complete names, places of birth, and dates of birth, marriage, and death. (You might also want to list burial sites.) Leave blanks for information you can't remember or don't know; perhaps you will be able to add it later.

Before you begin, look at the following example of a family tree.

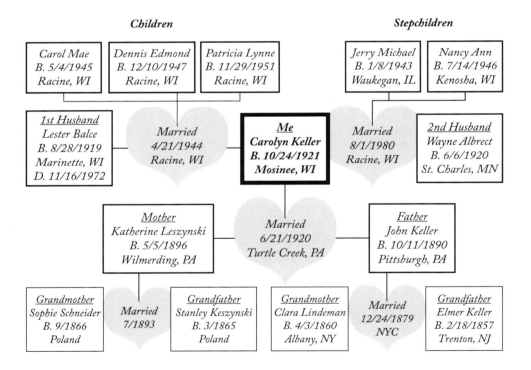

Children

Carol Mae B. 5/4/1945 Racine, WI	Dennis Edmond B. 12/10/1947 Racine, WI	Patricia Lynne B. 11/29/1951 Racine, WI

Stepchildren

Jerry Michael B. 1/8/1943 Waukegan, IL	Nancy Ann B. 7/14/1946 Kenosha, WI

1st Husband
Lester Balce
B. 8/28/1919
Marinette, WI
D. 11/16/1972

Married
4/21/1944
Racine, WI

Me
Carolyn Keller
B. 10/24/1921
Mosinee, WI

Married
8/1/1980
Racine, WI

2nd Husband
Wayne Albrect
B. 6/6/1920
St. Charles, MN

Mother
Katherine Leszynski
B. 5/5/1896
Wilmerding, PA

Married
6/21/1920
Turtle Creek, PA

Father
John Keller
B. 10/11/1890
Pittsburgh, PA

Grandmother
Sophie Schneider
B. 9/1866
Poland

Married
7/1893

Grandfather
Stanley Keszynski
B. 3/1865
Poland

Grandmother
Clara Lindeman
B. 4/3/1860
Albany, NY

Married
12/24/1879
NYC

Grandfather
Elmer Keller
B. 2/18/1857
Trenton, NJ

IN THE WORDS OF REAL PEOPLE

I was a little girl of 4, standing quietly, staring out to sea. The deck under my feet was slowly lifting and falling. "Why?" I wondered, "Did my mama and papa pack up everything and leave home?"

I was frightened now. Everyone else had the smallpox from having been scratched on the arm by that doctor before we left Sweden. It seemed everyone but me was sick.

They were afraid I would wander and fall into the ocean, so there was a rope around my waist, tied to a mast. I could no longer climb up the sails after the sailors. The captain was looking after me; he had become my friend.

I clung tightly to the little red box in my deep pocket, my very own tinderbox, given to me by my *farmoor*, my father's mother. How I wanted to go home! But Mama had said this was forever, a new home in a new land, across this big ocean. They said the crossing would take 3 months.

I would keep the red tinderbox forever. I would treasure it and the memories it brought of my grandmother in Sweden.
Myrt Grooms, *The Unraveling*

Whenever I begin researching our forefathers and their families, my emotions begin to kick in, and I feel the sorrow of them leaving their homeland on a journey fraught with danger and unknowns. The trip by ship in the 1800s and early 1900s was full of dangers, storms at sea, illness, human error, and ships that were not reliable. Why did they leave their homeland? Was it economic reasons? Was there a famine? Was there a breakdown in family life or hurt feelings? How did the mother and father that bid goodbye to their sons, daughters, and grandchildren handle the thought that they might never see their loved ones again? And often they did not . . . In the case of the Ericksons from Sweden, how did they feel leaving their beautiful, pristine Sweden? Or were their minds filled with stories of the thoughts of riches and land for the taking in the "New World"?
Norma Erickson, *Coming to a New Land*

My grandfather Leister Scholfield fought in our Civil War with the Michigan Volunteers. In the Battle of Chickamauga, he was shot in the chest and left on the battlefield as dead.

I have a copy of the letter written by his commanding officer to his father, Samuel, telling of his death. However, he was picked up by the Confederate forces and put in Libby Prison. He was given no medical attention except by fellow prisoners washing his wound with cold water. The bullet that wounded him lodged right next to his heart—too close for doctors of that era to attempt to remove it.

When Grandfather was released from the Army, he returned to his father's home, arriving in the late evening after doors were closed and locked. He knocked on the door. From inside he heard, "Who's there?" He answered, "Leister." His father, Samuel, having received the letter telling of Leister's death, asked from inside the house, "In the spirit? Or in the flesh?" To the joy of the household, Leister answered, "In the flesh."

Orren Gilbert Scholfield, *Many Cherries, Some Pits*

One day, as a young girl of 9, my mother, who was a newcomer to America from Italy, was shopping with her mother, who had need of a restroom. Now remember, my mother was just learning a new language. She saw a sign that read, "to let." She escorted her mother to the building where the printed sign was posted.

A gentleman answered the door and my mother pointed to the sign and said, "To let."

"Yes," said the gentleman, smiling. He showed them every room of the apartment and when he got to the bathroom my grandmother said "Grazie" and went in, closed the door, and relieved herself. It wasn't until sometime later that my mother could understand the confused look on the gentleman's face and chuckle about her mistake.

Benita Ackerman

YOU MAKE AN ENTRANCE

"A baby is God's opinion that life should go on." —Carl Sandburg

Now it's time to "get born." Think about the who, what, when, where, why, and how: remember to include as much detail as possible. Of course, many of our earliest moments are closed off to memory, so try and do some research—including talking to family or friends, if you can—to help fill in the blanks.

Our first memories are sometimes called "flash memories." We usually have two or three of them, which are like flashbulbs: isolated incidents, created when we were between 2 and 3 years old. These memories may come from out of the blue and appear very vivid. If you have any such memories, be sure to write them down!

- ❧ When and where were you born? Do you know anything about the birth itself?

- ❧ If you were adopted, tell about your first meeting with your parents. How much time did your parents have to prepare for your arrival? What else do you know about your adoption? When and how did you find out that you were adopted?

- ❧ Tell about your name. Do you know anything about your surname and its history? Why were you given your first name? Does it have any special meaning? Did you have any nicknames? Did you like or dislike your name or your nicknames?

- ❧ What stories do family members tell about your early years?

- ❧ Where did you live? What do you remember most about your home (or homes)? Was it in an urban or a rural area? How have you been influenced by the place of your early years?

●◆ Who came after you in your family? If you had younger brothers and sisters, tell about them. When were they born? How did you feel about their births?

●◆ Of all your relatives, to whom did you feel closest as a child? Why?

●◆ How much time did you spend with your grandparents? Do you have good memories of going to your grandmother's house? Which memory is your favorite? Did you spend time with your aunts and uncles and cousins?

●◆ What is your earliest remembered experience?

Place is something that many people use to define themselves. Some are comfortable only by water, while others love the desert. Some will miss trees if they move to the prairie, and others need to dwell in large urban areas. Think about yourself and the geographic place and climate that you most enjoy. Were you born in such a place? How did your birthplace affect the person you grew up to be?

WRITING TIPS

Keep your sentences and paragraphs short—all of us feel bogged down when we are faced with a half-page sentence or a three-page paragraph. You should also strive to avoid "elegant" words; simple words are more effective. For example, "fire" is a better choice than "conflagration." Finally, make sure to include information from all five senses—what did you see, hear, feel, taste, and smell?

> ## READING SUGGESTIONS
>
> ❧ "Some Things Don't Make Any Sense at All," from *If I Were in Charge of the World and Other Worries* by Judith Viorst—In this poem, Viorst wonders why in the world little brothers are born.
>
> ❧ *The Story of My Life* by Helen Keller—In the very first sentence of this straightforward autobiography, Keller confides that writing her story is difficult. It is a nice reassurance to all beginning writers.

MEMORY JOGGERS

"When you photograph people in color, you photograph their clothes. But when you photograph people in black and white, you photograph their souls!" —Ted Grant

Old pictures, scrapbooks, letters, programs, boxes of "junk": you might be amazed at how memory-provoking these items can be. Going through old mementos and photos can really help you get your memory juices flowing.

Old papers usually photocopy or scan well and you should consider including them in your story. Something you think is insignificant or silly might be fascinating to future generations. Go ahead and include a copy of an old report card, a ration book, or a certificate of achievement. Include old deeds, marriage licenses, citizenship papers, confirmation certificates, newspaper articles, school records, or any other official papers that might be of interest.

Photographs often scan reasonably well and will also add to your story. Include pictures of ancestors, baby pictures, childhood pictures, high school graduation pictures, wedding pictures, pictures of your children, and so on. Always identify the people in the pictures (including their first and last names), approximate dates, where the picture was taken, and any other relevant information that might apply.

One more memory jogger to consider is music. Listening to a recording of Glenn Miller, Frank Sinatra, Elvis Presley, the Rolling Stones, or Michael Jackson, for example, can release a flood of memories. CDs and MP3s are available of the top hits of every era, or, if you have them, simply get out your old vinyl records!

FLOOR PLAN

"Have nothing in your house that you do not know to be useful, or believe to be beautiful." —William Morris

Draw a floor plan of the house you grew up in. If you moved around a lot, draw the floor plan of the house you remember the most or of the house you lived in when you were 10 or 12.

Use a piece of graph paper or simply sketch the floor plan on ordinary paper. Put in rooms, closets, porches, as well as the big pieces of furniture that you recall: the kitchen table, the piano, the sofa, the stove. Some of you may even need to draw a path to the little house out back.

As you draw, try to remember the sights, sounds, smells, tastes, and feelings from this house. Perhaps you will smell sauerkraut, fresh-baked bread, barbecue ribs, or your father's pipe tobacco. Perhaps you will hear the squeaky board in the front hall, the old crystal set in the front room, the slam of the back screen door, or the neighbors in the apartment below. Perhaps you will feel the scratchy upholstery on the best overstuffed chair, the swish of beaded curtains, or the heat from the kitchen range as you get too close during your Saturday night bath. Perhaps you will see the back of your mother as she stands at the sink doing dishes, the family sitting down to Sunday dinner, or the jars and jars of peaches, pickles, and tomatoes lining the pantry shelves. Perhaps you will taste fresh picked fruit from the garden, your mother's homemade potato soup, or even a forbidden swig of bootleg whiskey.

You are likely to be surprised at the memories your floor plan arouses. Be sure to jot down notes about anything you might want to write about later. Then, as you continue to write about your memories, remember to be aware of the five senses and the feelings, thoughts, and emotions they evoke.

To help make your floor plan, I've provided an example.

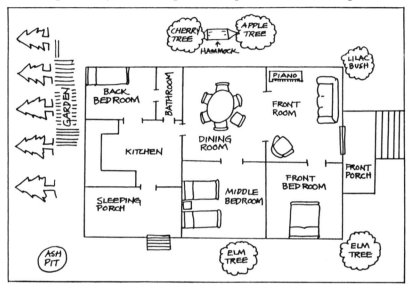

IN THE WORDS OF REAL PEOPLE

My foot touches the radiator under the kitchen window. It's a narrow kitchen and a narrower window. I lean forward at the waist, and my elbows touch the windowsill. The city comes to life in front of my eyes. The sun is burning down on the tar papered roofs across the street and far beyond. As I look north up Hudson Street to 9th Avenue, there is no horizon, just a massive confusion of steel and brick monoliths, which hem in the lower west side of Manhattan. One such building has a large neon sign on the roof —Nabisco. When the wind is right, the smell of cookies baking filters into my neighborhood.

My eyes slide down the sides of these buildings to the roofs of houses and tenements below. The hot sun has been beating down, melting the tar roofs and heating the brick until all you have to do is look at it and you can feel the heat. These tenements are from three stories to six stories high. My apartment is on the fifth floor of a six-story tenement, and I can look right across or down onto almost all the surrounding roofs.

My eyes slide down the walls of the tenements and over the fire escapes in a plunge to the streets below, where the trucks, buses, and cars come speeding south along 9th Avenue and down Hudson Street and past Horatio Street, where they pass out of sight around the corner of my tenement—50 Horatio Street.

There is movement on the third or fourth roof directly across from my kitchen window. The door on the roof opens and a young man steps out. He walks over to a cage on the roof and turns loose a flock of pigeons. He seems to circle something over his head and in a while the birds return to their nest.

This then was my domain. It was not mine alone, but embraced millions of children. Danger lurked on every roof, behind every window, around every corner. Excitement and adventure filled my every waking hour. No child has ever had a bigger or better playground. Any playground would pale next to the wonder that was New York City.

Ron Hildebrand, *Might as Well, Can't Dance*

The house had eight rooms (four bedrooms were upstairs and a bedroom for Mama and Dad was located on the first floor). A front room was used for storing feed and grain for the barnyard animals, and later it became the "parlor." There was a large dining room and a long table extended across the room. Two benches served as chairs, and they held about 16 people. Most of the time they were full; we seemed to have lots of company for meals.

The kitchen was located across the back of the house. A wood cookstove occupied its place of importance. There was a large icebox, and a rectangular work table stood in the middle of the room. There was no sink, no running water, not even a pump. An old-fashioned cupboard that had a built-in flour bin stood along an outer wall, and a woodbox rested in a corner near the doorway to the dining room.

I remember the aroma of brown sugar pies Mama made and stacked on the back of the stove as a special treat for us when we arrived home from school. Sometimes she put ears of corn in the oven to roast. She never let a warm day keep her from firing up the cookstove to make something for us. She knew we'd come home from school just starved!

Delia Grubb Martin, *Yesterday*

Shortly after we'd moved to the upper duplex next door to Grandpa George, my mother and father discovered the best bar in northeast Minneapolis, the Cactus Patch. It was here where a solid social core of northeast Minneapolis gathered nightly, and here my parents acquired instant friends they considered family. Children were welcomed, provided they sat quietly in a booth. The rules were: "No running allowed" and "Speak when spoken to."

The Cactus Patch got its name because the two store front windows, framing the exterior door, held every size and shape of cactus that flourished in miniature sand dunes on a simulated desert terrain. No one seemed to notice or care they were there. But I did. I loved the mysterious world of those plants that thrived on little water or sun.

Our frequent visits to the Cactus Patch began shortly after World War II broke out and continued well until the war was over. This became my second home, so I began bringing my books along. I studied and completed homework assignments under a yellow light in a back corner booth. When I was done, I'd watch endless games of cribbage and eventually learned to calculate every combination of 15 possible. I came to know that what followed 10 was not necessarily 11 but could be the jack, queen, or king. By the time I was in third grade, I knew how to bid and win eight of any suit in 500 and frequently was asked to sit in as a fourth hand. Over the months and years, I witnessed individuals debate political, social, and personal events over ice cubes and a swizzle stick. And I pondered existential questions, such as what larger destiny life had in store for all of us, despite the elusive rantings of people who thought they could solve the problems of the world from the vantage point of a bar stool.

Donna Davis, *Dancing in the Cactus Patch*

BEING A CHILD

"I look in the mirror through the eyes of the child that was me." —Judy Collins

What was it like to be a child? What do you fondly recall? What do you not-so-fondly recall? It may be difficult, but try to remember how you spent your time growing up— the good, the bad, the annoying, or the just plain silly. In school or at home, with friends or alone, think back to your early years, from birth until about age 12.

- Describe yourself as a child. What did you look like? How did you dress? How did you wear your hair?

- Think about your behavior and your general demeanor. Were you shy or boisterous? An angel or a menace? Was there a difference between what others said you were like and what you felt like inside?

- What do you remember with real pleasure from your childhood? Tell about a good time you had growing up.

- What did you do for fun? What games did you play?

- Did you participate in any pranks or daring escapades, risky business, or narrow escapes as a child?

- What did you want to be when you grew up? Did you have any goals at that age?

- How did you spend your days? Describe a typical day in the springtime, the summer, the autumn, and the winter when you were 9 or 10 years old. What did summertime mean to you as a child?

- Describe the conditions and attitudes of your family and neighbors during the historic period of time you grew up in: the Depression, the World War II years, the Cold War years of the 1950s, the turbulence of the 1960s, or more recent decades. How did the events of your childhood years affect you and your family?

●◆ Was anyone outside of your family very special to you when you were growing up? Why? How?

●◆ When you reflect on your childhood, do you recall a gathering place where you and your family relaxed, talked, or shared an activity?

●◆ What were the communication and entertainment equipment, the appliances, and the primary mode of transportation like during your childhood?

●◆ How did your family take part in the life of your community? Were family members active in church or school affairs? What about clubs, sports, politics or cultural events? Explain.

There is a big difference between being 5 years old and being 10 years old. There is not as big a difference between being 37 and 42 years old, though that, too, is a five-year time span. Think about how wonderful it would be for you if you had written memories of your great-grandparents' childhood activities and the games they played at that time in their lives. Think back to those years, between the ages of 5 and 10, and write down as much as you can about your favorite pastimes and how they developed and changed.

WRITING TIPS

Including dialogue in your autobiography is usually a very effective technique. Of course you can't recreate the exact words of a conversation that took place years ago, but you can use dialogue to create a general sense of what happened. Because people are always interested in what others have to say, the use of dialogue will make your writing more interesting to read.

READING SUGGESTIONS

●◆ *This House of Sky: Landscapes of a Western Mind* by Ivan Doig— Doig's autobiography is a lyrically written book about growing up in Montana during the Great Depression without a mother and with a father who did the best he could.

●◆ *Growing Up* by Russell Baker—Baker writes about what life was like living on the East Coast during the 1930s. He notes that his children will want to know "how it was to be young in the time before jet planes, super-highways, H-bombs and the global village of television."

IN THE WORDS OF REAL PEOPLE

From the time Mom and Dad married in 1923 until Dad had his first heart attack, about 1943, he worked as a milk-man for Meadow Gold Dairy (Beatrice Creamery Company). In the early years, he would leave about 1 a.m. and go to the dairy and load up his horse and wagon. This consisted of slinging 60-pound cases of milk from the dock into his wagon; loading butter, ice cream, etc., which were packed in dry ice in the summer; and making his deliveries before daylight. Then he would begin collecting, door-to-door, and return home about 1 p.m.

Most of his route consisted of apartments and, in many instances, he would take the dairy products inside and put them in the old ice boxes. Most people didn't lock their doors then, and those who did often gave him a key if they would not be there. He also delivered to a lot of bakeries, restaurants, and grocery stores. Because he ate breakfast out every day—and was in the kitchens of so many restaurants—he would never, never take Mom or any of us out to eat. He said if we saw what he had seen in the kitchens, we wouldn't want to eat out either.

Once when I was probably about 5, or younger, my dad took me to work with him. After he loaded up, we headed up to East Denver, which was his route. It was very dark, and probably the first time I had ever been up that early in the morning. I had never ridden in an electric truck before, and I can remember still how astonished I was when Dad came to his first stop, turned off the ignition, jumped out the door, and went running up to deliver the milk. The truck didn't stop, and I was scared to death. In truth, it only went a few feet and then stopped, but those few seconds seemed an eternity to me. When Dad came back, he explained to me that when you turn off an electric motor, it has to run down—it doesn't stop immediately.

Clare Foster, *Roses and Thorns*

I do remember the dust storms. The wind blew constantly, night and day, and the air was so full of dust it blotted out the sun. Dust was everywhere; a coat of dust would be on the dining room table when we got up in the morning. My mother would push strips of cloth around the windows, but it still sifted in. Sometimes it was difficult to breathe. We played indoors during the bad storms, in the house or in the hayloft of the barn. The dust was very hard on livestock, as it got into their noses and they had trouble breathing. Sometimes it would get so dark the chickens would go to roost, thinking it was night. When there wasn't a storm, it would be hot and dry with not a cloud in the sky. I can remember clouds forming, and everyone's prayer was for rain. But it seldom rained during those years.

Then, when you thought it couldn't get any worse, the hoards of grasshoppers began. They appeared like a huge cloud in the sky. They ate every blade of living vegetation until there was nothing left . . . corn and wheat would be stalks in the field. I hated and feared grasshoppers. They were large brown insects, and they flew in the car windows and invariably hit me right on the forehead. Their brown juice would run down my face, and I would stand and scream. My mother would stop the car, get out, catch the grasshopper, wipe off my face, and we would continue.

Mary Skuderna

Frisk was his name; frisky he was. This good-sized, black and white dog didn't need a pedigree, for he knew he was something special. He ruled our yard. No one came or went or crossed it without his knowing about it—and approving. He also was special, especially to Dad. He knew always, day or night, where Dad was around our house: yard, garden, chicken coops, goat shed, Jersey-cow enclosure, or barn.

And Dad reciprocated—he liked to have that ol' dog dog-gin' his heels.

Frisk made it a habit to accompany Dad to church each Sunday. Dad went early to Lead Belt Presbyterian Church, usually about 7 or 8 a.m., to let fresh air in, stir up the furnace on cold Sundays and clean up, if need be, for the 9:45 Sunday school and 11 a.m. service—our small church couldn't afford a paid janitor. Frisk dutifully waited outside for Dad and our family to start the half-mile trek home after church. All of our Presbyterians recognized and appreciated Frisk's unfailing attendance at church.

Then, in 1929, our family took the old Model T Ford touring car for a week-long trip as far as the New York World's Fair and Niagara Falls. Ol' Frisk was left at home. Upon returning, as we got back to church, we joked with friends, "Well, this is one time ol' Frisk didn't go to Sunday school."

"You must be kidding," was the rejoinder. "Frisk was right here at church last Sunday."

Wally Stewart

YOUR MEMORIES
ARE YOUR OWN

"Life is not what one lived, but what one remembers and how one remembers it in order to recount it." —Gabriel García Márquez

Remember that your life story is indeed your story, not the story of your parents, siblings, children, or spouse. You need to write about events from your own point of view, as you remember them.

People who are writing their life story often become intimidated by others. An older brother or sister may read a chapter and say, "That didn't happen that way at all!" An aunt or uncle may laugh at a "wrong" description of a family get-together.

Remember that it is natural and normal for people to have different memories about the same event. Brothers and sisters especially, usually because of age differences, recall the past in sometimes startlingly different ways. That's all right. Each individual writes an autobiography from his or her own perspective, not from the perspective of anyone else. Let those who recall things differently write their own autobiographies!

WRITING TIPS

An autobiography is a personal journey. It cannot and should not be the story of a person's brothers or sisters. However, siblings play a large role in a person's early years, and readers always want to know what became of them. At some point, be sure to write a paragraph or two about your siblings as adults, briefly filling out the rest of the story, and include photos of them both as children and as older adults. In other words, don't lose them!

IN THE WORDS OF REAL PEOPLE

When we got to the pond, my sister Marie sat down and began to take off her shoes and stockings. I begged her not to do it: "You know Dad wouldn't want you to. You'll get muddy splashes on your new dress."

Nothing worked. I got mad and shouted, "Just go ahead. I don't care what happens to you. I wish I hadn't finished your new dress! I'll never do anything for you again!"

Getting no reply, I turned to look back. She was gone. I was scared. I didn't know where she was. I didn't want to go into the water, but she wasn't on the land. Then I saw her head surface.

I was afraid of the water, but everything I'd ever heard about drowning flashed through my head. I hadn't been watching; I didn't know whether this was the first or last time she'd come to the surface. But I had to get her out. To this day, I do not know how I did it, but I dragged her to shore. Then I got sick. When I straightened up, she was being sick, too. I turned her over and held her head so she could spit it out.

Part of me died in that pond. I had nightmares about that day from then on.

This is a story whose lasting mystery was cleared up only after I worked on writing my autobiography. My sister and I have been at loggerheads ever since that day when she was 15 years old and I saved her life. She always hovered over me, trying to fix this or that, telling me a better way to do something, seeing if I was properly dressed when I went out, etc. I resented that greatly.

She recently called from California where she is in a nursing home near her oldest daughter, and we were talking about writing our autobiographies. She said, "Are you going to tell about the pond story?"

"Well, that's your story," I answered.

"If you hadn't been there, I wouldn't have had any story," she said. "I still don't think I've paid you for it. I've always tried to do everything I could, but I still think my life is yours."

"What on Earth are you talking about?" I asked.

"You know, the Indian belief: If you save a life, the person saved is responsible for the other forever after. I guess I'm more Indian than I look."

And here, for 70 years, I had thought she was just picking on me because she was my older sister!

Viola Smith, Here I Am

SCHOOL DAYS

"Children today are tyrants. They contradict their parents, gobble their food, and tyrannize their teachers." —Socrates

Much of childhood life is dominated by that venerated educational institution known as school. At what age did you start going to school? Did you enjoy it? Did you make friends? What did you like about school? What did you dislike? Here are some questions to help you think about your days in the classroom:

- Describe your grade school. What was it like? What were your favorite subjects? What school programs do you remember? Which teachers stand out in your mind?

- Did your school include first through eighth grades, or were there separate elementary and middle or junior high schools? Did you attend kindergarten? Was there a graduation ceremony at the finish of elementary school?

- How did you feel about school? Was school generally a pleasant or unpleasant experience for you? What kind of student were you?

- How did you get to school? Describe your daily trip.

- Did you learn public speaking in school? Was that painful or easy? Did you learn a specific method of reading or writing? Did you participate in spelling bees?

- Did you go home for lunch, bring your lunch to school, or eat school lunch?

- What did you do during recess? Did your activities differ from fall to winter to spring?

- Were you ever sent to the principal's office? Why? What happened?

- Did you experience any schoolyard bullying?

- How did your school day change as you got older? When you got to junior high, how did your schedule differ? Was it for better or for worse?

- Were you in plays or orchestra? Did you participate in athletics? Were you a crossing guard?

- Did you have to memorize information such as state capitals, multiplication tables, poems, the periodic table of elements, or names of U. S. Presidents?

- Did you take home economics, industrial arts, or computer/typing classes? Did your school offer classes in music, art, and gym? Did you learn any foreign languages?

- Did you come to school knowing English? If not, was that difficult?
- What did you do when school was over? Where did you go? What did you do?

Our memories are organized by categories: the first memory of a topic, place, or event is often the most vivid and then similar memories are put in that box or file of memory category. For example, the first day of each school year is more memorable, more vivid than the 32nd day. Think about the first day of school each year. Did you typically find yourself filled with anticipation and excitement, or dread and worry?

READING SUGGESTIONS

- *Nothing Daunted: The Unexpected Education of Two Society Girls in the West* by Dorothy Wickenden—This book is derived from the letters of two college-educated young women from very privileged families of upstate New York who taught in a country schoolhouse to homesteader children in northwest Colorado in 1916 and 1917. The teachers are amazed at the resilience and fortitude of the homesteaders, whose hardships included a 5-mile horseback ride to school in deep snow during the worst winter in years.
- *The Life and Times of the Thunderbolt Kid: A Memoir* by Bill Bryson—Bryson relates the many humorous experiences of one very mischievous boy growing up in Iowa in the 1950s.

GROWING PAINS

"A person's a person, no matter how small." —Dr. Seuss

As children grow older, they quickly learn that life isn't all fun and games. In many ways, childhood can be the toughest time of all. You get hurt; you feel shame. You start to understand the world that exists outside your home, and it is not always easy or pleasant. Recall some of the less happy moments of your growing-up years, and remember: be honest with yourself! Know that what you are writing and the insights and thoughts you are providing your family with will be profoundly cherished.

- What was distressing during your childhood years? Did you experience the death of a loved one, a natural disaster, an illness, or an accident of some kind? Tell about a difficult time growing up. Did you ever get into trouble? Tell about a mischievous thing you did as a child. Who was the major disciplinarian in your family, your mother or your father? How were you disciplined as a child? For what?

- Was anyone ever mean to you? How did you handle it?

- Were you ever quite sick as a child? Did you break any bones or have an operation or need stitches? What was your medical care like?

- Did your family, friends, or neighbors have any folk remedies for illnesses when you were small? If so, describe them.

- When and how did you learn to read? How did that make you feel?

- Who taught you to tie your shoes? To make your bed? To cook or to repair a car?

- Who taught you manners and how to get along with others?

- When you lost a tooth when you were little, what happened?

- Did you have a secret as a child—a secret hiding place, a secret friend or some other secret? Explain.

➻ Did you have to do any chores as a youngster? How did you feel about that?

A wonderful opportunity arises when recalling youth: you can talk about your values (both family and personal) without ever having to shake that parent finger! Think about the messages you'd like to send in your writing, and how you can illustrate "shoulds" and "should nots" without explicitly saying so. The pen bestows great power—wield it responsibly!

WRITING TIPS

Have you ever skipped a smooth, flat stone in a clear pond? As it hits the water, the stone makes ripples around the point of impact. Then it skips, and more ripples appear.

You can help generate ripples in your mind whenever you want to remember details about a particular subject. Try this: Write the name of the subject in the center of a page. Focus on that subject and draw "ripples" out from it, jotting down any detail at all that you can remember. Each ripple can then generate ripples of its own. Soon you will have a whole page of memories, and it will be easy to begin writing.

The following graphic is an example of one woman's ripples, as she focused on the subject of her mother.

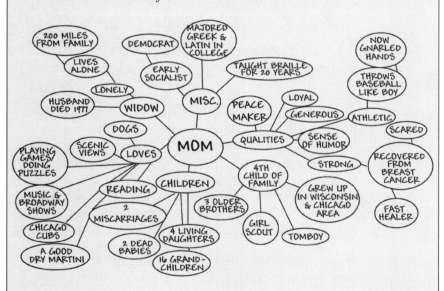

Now do some rippling of your own. Try one of the following topics, or another of your choice:

- your father
- school
- the 1990s
- sibling rivalry
- pets
- loves

READING SUGGESTIONS

•➻ *One Writer's Beginnings* by Eudora Welty—Welty writes about her happy childhood, describing in great detail the events and people that contributed to her future as a fiction writer.

IN THE WORDS OF REAL PEOPLE

Mother was the one who dealt out the discipline at our house, and her word was law. She was very strict and expected perfection. One thing that Mother would not tolerate was lying or stealing. At school we had an arrangement with one of the banks where we would have a real savings book from the bank. Each week, or maybe it was every 2 weeks, Mother would give my sister Osa and me 5 cents to put in the bank. This money was not to be spent without Mother's approval.

One day we decided to spend 2 cents for candy at the grocery store on the corner of the school yard and only deposit 3 cents. We didn't think Mother would ever know the difference.

The bank book came home with our report cards, and there were all of the 5-cent entries and then this glaring 3-cent entry. Mom had been around the block a couple of times and knew what had happened. She slept on it. The next morning when she was combing our hair for school, she asked about it. Can you believe we both lied to her? I was in the second grade and Osa was in the fourth. We were old enough to know better. (I probably talked Osa into buying the candy. It wasn't like her to do something like that.) It is the only time I can remember her spanking us with a razor strap instead of a yard stick. She was so mad that she really laid it on us.

We were both crying on our way to school. It was winter, and I can remember taking snow and rubbing our eyes with it, so the kids at school wouldn't know we had been crying.

                              Julia L. "Judy" Graham, *My Life*

Our behavior in school was strictly regimented. When the teacher spoke, we were to sit up straight with our feet together and our hands clasped on top of the desk, eyes on the teacher. Talking amongst ourselves was never permitted in class. Morning and afternoon, we had an activity which was delicately referred to as Health. When it came time for Health, we formed two lines and proceeded to the basement, where we all took turns going to the bathroom. When we finished, we took our places in line again and returned to the classroom.

Sally Howard, *Work in Progress*

When I was young, the main fuel that we had to burn was cow chips (cow manure). Every fall we would take a team and wagon and go out in the pastures and pick them up. We usually drug an old tub or something to gather them in, and then we dumped them in the wagon. We could usually get two loads a day. We would bring the chips home and pile them up for winter. I guess you could tell how enterprising a homesteader was by the pile of chips that he had. It saved many a person from the cold.

I remember one time when we had a bad blizzard and one of the neighbors ran out of fuel. He took a hand saw and went out to his fences and sawed the posts off above the wire. For many years you could see where he had done that. I guess he thought that he still would have his fence, and I am sure that he needed the fuel to keep his family from freezing to death.

Fred Wurtsmith, *It's Been a Long Road*

When I was 10 or 11, there occurred a case of incest in our town. My dad was a lawyer, and the court appointed him to represent the father. Much discussion took place in our house in hushed tones, which naturally aroused my curiosity. I asked what was going on, and my mother took a stab at enlightening me.

She said, "John, you know what you have down there," and gestured rather vaguely toward my lower abdomen. I don't recall what else she said, but it must have been pretty murky. All I know is that I was suspicious and perplexed about my belly button for some time.

John Mills

One fall at school they had a "thing" going about tonsillitis, and the county nurse decided that anyone living as far as we did from a doctor should have their tonsils out, whether they had a history of sore throats or not. They must have been very persuasive because it was decided that three of the Phillips' kids should have their tonsils out—my older brother Roy, my older sister Jane, and me.

After the three tonsillectomies, Dad and we three kids walked 14 blocks to the train depot, boarded the train, rode the 35 miles to the Decker switch, got off the train and walked the half mile home, the only instruction being not to run and start our throats to bleeding. Our Aunt Bertha was so mad she could have eaten a goatburger. She told over and over again about Dad taking three of his kids to have their tonsils out, and they never even missed a milkin'.

Charles A. Phillips, *Dryland Diary*

WRITING ON THE DARK SIDE

"Memory is not just the imprint of the past time upon us; it is the keeper of what is meaningful for our deepest hopes and fears." —Rollo May

Fortunately for us, memories tend to be pleasant. If we remembered only the unpleasant, our mental institutions would be jam-packed.

Many adults, however, have memories of historical horrors like the Holocaust, Japanese internment camps, and the Vietnam War. These historical horrors seem to be easier to write about than personal tragedies, perhaps because they are well-documented and publicly shared by many men and women.

It is much more difficult to write about personal, private horrors: sexual abuse, the mental illness of a close family member, the death of a child, the alcoholism of a parent, or the unfaithfulness of a spouse. Personal horrors almost always involve other people, and writers are often hesitant to write something that they think is private, something that they think might hurt someone else.

Difficult though it may be, it is important to write about the dark side of life. Here are some suggestions that may help you:

- Remember that life is not a sugar-coated pill. You will be doing your descendants an injustice if you ignore the unpleasant side of life. In writing your autobiography, you have an opportunity to share with your children, grandchildren, and great-grandchildren the wisdom you have gained from surviving hard times, deep personal hurts, and/or devastating losses.

- Write from your own perspective. You cannot presume to write about the lives of others or about their feelings, but you can write about your own reactions to people and events. More importantly, you can write about how you survived, what sustained you, and what gave you strength and hope.

- Remember that you don't have to share everything you write. You can tell about your worst memories honestly, writing as if no one else will ever read your words. You can decide later what to include and what to leave out of your book. You will be glad you wrote with candor, even if you decide to include very little in the end.

- Remember that writing about the dark side of life can be therapeutic. Putting words of bile and bitterness on paper often results in deeper understanding. Writing truthfully can help you discover truths about yourself and about other relationships.

IN THE WORDS OF REAL PEOPLE

At Dulag Luft, the German interrogation center, I was placed in solitary. I was interrogated by a Luftwaffe officer who spoke good English. He told me he had been to Wichita. He did not press me much for information; in fact, he told me more about our groups than I knew. After interrogation, I was taken out of solitary and used in the kitchen to peel potatoes. Also, I was allowed to write a short letter to my folks. (This letter was not received by them until March 31, 1944. My folks received wire from the Adjutant General on January 11, 1944, stating I was a prisoner of war.)

There were about 80 enlisted men who had been processed to be sent to a prisoner of war camp. We were loaded into two small box cars. (During World War I, this size of car was referred to as 40 and 8; i.e., 40 men, 8 horses.) Each end of the car had a deck about 30 inches above the floor. In the center of the car they had a sand box and a container where a fire could be built to help to keep the car from getting so cold. Our train spent a lot of time on side tracks so other trains could pass. I don't recall how we were fed, or if we were let out of the car on any of the stops. I do recall trying to relieve myself out the boxcar door while the train was moving. I had to have another person hold me so as not to be thrown out. Dennis and I slept on the floor beneath the second deck. This gave us enough room to actually lay down.

Our train arrived at Krems, Austria, about midnight on December 10 and we walked to Stalag 17-B, a distance of about three or four miles.

Dean Sommers

I believe it was his first year of teaching at our school, and I don't know if he had a family somewhere. Our home became his home-away-from-home on occasion. He was a rather portly man with a blushing face. He liked for me to sit on his lap, and at such times he would perform touching indiscretions, which made me uneasy. I was not yet 6 years old, and it was definitely an act of sexual abuse. I am sure my sister did not know this side of him, but at the time, I wanted her to protect me, yet I was afraid to tell. Another time a boy tried to pull my underpants, and I told the principal. When it got around to the teachers, Miss Bessie turned on me, asking, "Why did you tell?" I don't think teachers were equipped to handle sexual abuse and, indeed, didn't want to be involved. It was a subject I learned not to talk about and, I believe, contributed to my reluctance to speak out when serious problems needed to be resolved. Who would listen?

Delia Grubb Martin, Yesterday

WHAT IN THE WORLD IS ISINGLASS?

"I pretty much try to stay in a constant state of confusion just because of the expression it leaves on my face." —*Johnny Depp*

When writing about your life, remember to explain what you mean. Your grandchildren may be mystified by words and phrases that are common knowledge to your generation.

Take the time to explain terms that might not be familiar to younger readers: terms like *isinglass*, *the WPA*, *air-raid drills*, *McCarthyism*, *Sputnik*, *flower children*, *cassette tapes*, and *Y2K*, to name just a few. Also remember that the meanings of words can change over time. Words like *pot, grass, gay*, and *coke,* for example, have taken on new meanings in the last 50 years.

The following selection from "Milkmen Lost in Generation Gap" by Guernsey Le Pelley illustrates how little young readers often know about day-to-day life in the first half of the 20th century.

> Several days ago I fell into a generation gap. I try not to fall into them more than once a week, but sometimes I run over. I was talking to a 10-year-old friend about my father. In the conversation I said, "His best friend was a milkman."
>
> "A what?" said the youngster.
>
> "A milkman," I answered matter-of-factly.
>
> "What was he? Made out of milk?"
>
> This kid seemed a bit stupid. "No," I said flatly. "He delivered milk. Also butter and eggs. Like the iceman delivered ice!"
>
> The kid's eyes glazed over. "People carried milk and eggs and ice around? For what?"
>
> Evidently this is what happens. Whole pieces of social planking drop out of the structure of history. I can remember milkmen clearly. I can even remem-

ber they were the last to give up horses for delivery, because going along a street the horse remembered which house to stop at better than the milkman did.

I could see the youngster really didn't know what I was talking about, so I explained. "People left a note at the door saying how many bottles they wanted."

"Bottles?"

"Yes, bottles. Milk came in bottles. The milkman would pick up the empties, put them in the rack he carried and leave full ones. Then the people would bring them in and take the cream off . . ."

"Cream? There was a bottle of cream stacked on top of the bottle of milk?"

"No," I said patiently. "The cream was in the milk. The top half of the bottle . . ."

I could see this was slightly confusing information, so I didn't bother to introduce ragmen to the conversation. Neither did I mention scissor-grinders, who came around fairly often to sharpen our kitchen knives. But I couldn't let him off too easily.

"Later on in the day," I said, giving him something to think about, "the waffleman came by. I could get a crisp, freshly cooked waffle, covered with powered sugar, for a penny."

When I left, the kid was talking to a friend and pointing in my direction—probably telling him I was from another planet.

And I guess I was.

SPECIAL TIMES

"We love to expect, and when expectation is either disappointed or gratified, we want to be again expecting." —Samuel Johnson

Every childhood includes special times, whether they are holidays, family celebrations, or meaningful occasions of a personal nature. These occasions usually involve a great deal of anticipation, especially during childhood. Was there ever a birthday or Christmas when you did not receive a gift you had desperately hoped for? Be sure to include not just your fondest memories, but stories of disappointment, too, so the children in your life will understand these kinds of feelings are normal and okay to have. Use these questions to help you remember special times from your childhood:

- How did your family celebrate holidays? Is there one particular holiday you remember especially well? Why?

- What were some of your family traditions? Did they include extended family members, like grandparents, aunts, uncles and cousins?

- What special foods did your family like to prepare? Did your mother or father make any holiday treats?

- What was the best gift you ever received when you were young? What was the best gift you ever gave?

- What birthday do you remember best? Why?

- Did you go on vacations with your family? Where did you go? How did you get there?

- Did you ever attend a circus, major league baseball game, vaudeville show, revival meeting, Broadway play, carnival, amusement park, or other exciting event when you were young? Describe what you saw and how you felt.

➔ Did you attend any funerals as a child? How did you and your family cope?

➔ Do you remember any "firsts" from childhood—first Communion, first trip to the movies, first haircut, etc.?

There are three parts to every special occasion. The first part is planning and anticipation— and for a child, we all know how this time went *so* slowly! The second part of a special event is the event itself, to be enjoyed to the maximum (or sometimes to be dreadfully disappointed by). And the third part is the remembering, which is what you as a writer are engaging in now. Each part of a special event is equally important; the anticipation, the event itself, and the remembering. Make sure to address each aspect as you write about your special moments.

WRITING TIPS

As you write your memoirs, keep in mind these two words: *facts* and *anecdotes*. Facts will help your readers understand the basics: how people, places, and events shaped your life. Facts are very important, but anecdotes will keep your readers interested and entertained.

Think about the amusing, unusual, uncomfortable, triumphant, frightening, poignant, ridiculous, and radiant moments of your life. What stories can you tell about these moments?

If you have not yet informed your siblings or cousins that you are writing down the stories of your life, you might think about doing so. The special times of childhood are usually special because they were shared with so many others and you may need to check facts with others so you can add the anecdotes with confidence!

READING SUGGESTIONS

➥ *All I Really Need to Know I Learned in Kindergarten* by Robert Fulghum—In his essay that begins "And speaking of gifts . . ." Fulghum muses about the connection between gifts and thoughts, concluding that what most adults want for Christmas is simply to be 5 years old again.

IN THE WORDS OF REAL PEOPLE

November 1 used to be a major holiday in New Orleans. Schools closed, florists stocked up on chrysanthemums, and we all went to the cemeteries to honor our dead on All Saint's Day. Everything had to be in perfect order on November 1 because the whole city would be there to pass judgment if you neglected your ancestors. This was the one day of the year when the entire McLellan family met.

My great-great-grandfather, William Henry Paine McLellan, had bought a large chunk of the cemetery for the use of his descendants. My great-great-grandfather was from Maine, and he came to New Orleans in about 1840. His sons fought for the Confederacy, and one of them, Charles, was killed at Meadow Bridge near Richmond in 1864. After the war, his father went to Virginia and brought the body home for burial. At that time, it was impossible to bury the dead in the ground, because of the high water table in New Orleans, but to my great-great-grandfather, that was the only civilized form of burial. The McLellan Mound made it possible for his family to be laid under 6 feet of earth. The mound is a raised area, probably 4–5 feet high, surrounded by a granite coping with a small iron picket fence on top. (I have cousins who claim that the dirt was imported from Maine so that he could be buried in Maine soil, but I can't believe that a thrifty Yankee of Scottish extraction would have indulged in such an expensive flight of sentiment.)

Every year at the cemetery, in addition to social chit-chat, I heard the same stories. How, when Captain Charles was killed, two young ladies went in deep mourning for him, each one believing that she was his fiancée. (Aunt Stel said three, but Aunt Stel always wanted to make a good story.)

We heard about my great-great-grandmother, Leonora Levansaler (Captain Charles' mother). During the occupation of New Orleans, she used to lower her parasol in front of her face as she walked, making it necessary for Yankee soldiers to step off the sidewalk to let her go by . . .

One of the most famous tombs is of red marble. The statue in front of it is of a young girl knocking at the door of the tomb. It originally belonged to the madam of an extremely successful brothel. There is a story that she got her start in business one night when she arrived home so late that her father had locked the door against her. At one time, a number of people claimed to have seen the tomb glowing with an eerie red light that could not reasonably be explained.

Sally Howard, *Work in Progress*

When I was in school, one time we had a music contest, and our teacher thought that I should sing a solo in this contest. I was about the third one to sing.

As the teacher started beating on the piano, I started singing, "Twilight is falling over all." I looked down and saw my mother, and something blanked me out. I quit singing. I just couldn't come up with another word of any kind. The teacher started beating on the piano again, and I started over. "Twilight is falling over all," I sang. I quit again. The third time it was, "Twilight is falling over all," again, and I walked off the stage.

There were seven of us in that contest. My coach saw me out in the hall later. He came up to me and said, "Ivan, you did well. After six, you came in first."

Ivan Klein, *The Autobiography of Ivan Klein*

Winnie Morgan was, and still is, a dear friend of mine. As a child she was giggly, good-natured, and chubbier than any kid in Lone Star. One year when we were children, we attended a revival meeting.

Revival meetings were held at High Point for two weeks during the winter. An evangelist would come and stay with a family or two. He was always a powerful singer, and sometimes other singers would come and sing with him. They'd dramatize the songs and make a "sinner" like I was at 12 years old feel so guilty that I knew if I didn't go forward, the devil would get me before I got home.

The song "Just as I Am," played and sung over and over, convinced me that I was good enough for the Lord to want. As my good, lifetime friend Winnie Morgan and I knelt at that special time in our lives to be baptized by sprinkling, Winnie got tickled. She whispered to me, "I'm wetting my pants." She wasn't joking.

The big stain was on the floral carpet for years to come. She and I would sometimes, together, go up to the front of the church and check on it.

Helen Tisdel

In the second grade, I had a good friend named Clark. At times, he would walk home from school with me. In those days, alleyways were an important part of every city block. Incinerators for the burning of trash were placed in alleyways, and the garages were toward the back of the property with an alley entrance. It was in one particular alley that I received my first kiss on the lips! Clark was the giver of that first kiss, and we liked it so well that we tried a couple more!

Janet Williamson, *My Story*

FAVORITES

"I don't believe in 'greatest.' I believe in favorites." —Steve Vai

Favorites make up a big part of who we are. We use them to identify like-minded people, and they often play a role in how we present ourselves to the world. Favorites can change over time; as a child, you may have had many more favorites than you do now. Think about some of the following topics, and try to remember the things that you liked most:

- ❖ What were some of your favorite bedtime stories?

- ❖ Do you remember any favorite childhood poems, games, or songs?

- ❧ As a child, did you ever collect anything? What? Which was your favorite in the collection?

- ❧ How about favorite movies? Books? Toys? Comics? Describe them.

- ❧ Who were your heroes when you were a child? Why?

- ❧ As a child, what did you wish for? Was there a recurring wish you made every year as you blew out your birthday candles?

- ❧ What were your fantasies?

- ❧ What was your favorite color? Why did you like it? Did it ever change?

- ❧ What kind of foods did your family make? Did you have a favorite meal? If you have any family recipes, you should consider including them in your autobiography!

Reading biographies and autobiographies of other people is a worthwhile activity for an autobiographical writer. Pay attention to the author's style of writing and to why some biographies or autobiographies are more interesting than others. An author's life may not be more interesting than any other, but the style of writing can make it seem so. Experiment with different styles to see which one best suits you.

WRITING TIPS

When you are writing, try to avoid the frequent use of clichés: worn-out phrases like "nipped in the bud," "wise as an owl," "the old college try," "clear as a bell," and countless others. Make up fresh, new phrases to describe your experiences.

Here are some examples:

- ❧ "A rainbow is happy dancing ribbons in the sky." —Ethan Borg

- ❧ "Music was my refuge. I could crawl into the spaces between the notes and curl my back to loneliness." —Maya Angelou, *Singin' and Swingin' and Gettin' Merry Like Christmas*

READING SUGGESTIONS

∞ *Old Ways Rediscovered* by Clarence Meyer—This fascinating book is full of old remedies, beauty tips, and herbal recipes and potions.

∞ "How to Write a Novel About Your Family" by Vincent Lam—Author Vincent Lam writes about the research he put into writing his novel *The Headmaster's Wager,* which was inspired by his grandfather's adventures in 1960s Saigon. Though his novel is fictional, much of Lam's advice can be applied to auto-biographical writing; of particular note are his comments on perspective and tone. The article can be accessed online for free at http://www.publishersweekly.com/pw/by-topic/book-news/tip-sheet/article/53503-how-to-write-a-novel-about-your-family.html.

TIMELINE

"The stories unfolding in front of me—the civil rights movement, Vietnam, the race to the moon—were matched by stories developing within me." —Daniel Taylor

Adults can't help but be affected by the historical events of their lives. For example, the Depression of the 1930s had a profound influence upon anyone who lived through it. So did World War II, Kennedy's assassination, and the events of September 11, 2001. We have all been affected by the social changes and upheavals of the past 60 years—civil rights, women's equality, the sexual revolution, gay liberation, the rising divorce rate, etc.

Although all of us are affected by history, each of us is also a history maker, contributing to the history of spouses and children, neighbors, friends, and coworkers. Many people influence the history of the nation or of the world—for example, suffragettes of the early 20th century, prohibitionists, soldiers of World War II, civil rights demonstrators of the 1950s and 1960s, or the environmentalists in the 1980s. (Almanacs include excellent history sections that touch on the important events of each year.)

Making a timeline is an interesting way to put your life in historical perspective. To create a timeline, first make three columns and title them "My Life," "Date," and "World Events," respectively. In the left-hand column, list all of the milestones of your life, starting with your birth. In the middle column, record the date of each milestone. In the right-hand column, jot down what was taking place on the national or international scene at that time. (Use your local library or the Internet for research. You might include information about wars, the economy, politics, social upheavals, and other events.)

For the milestones in your life, you might want to include the following:

- going to school for the first time,
- graduating from eighth grade or junior high,
- moving,
- entering high school,
- graduating from high school,
- entering military service,
- entering college,
- graduating from college,
- getting married,
- births and deaths of loved ones,
- times of serious illness and/or crisis, and/or
- times of personal success and achievement.

Your finished timeline will show how your life is intertwined with the history of the United States and the world. It is also an interesting way to help your children and grandchildren understand how we are all shaped by the times in which we live. The example that follows shows one writer's timeline.

My Life	Date	World Events
Born	September, 1939	World War II begins in Europe
Start school	September, 1945	World War II ends; Hiroshima bombed
Move to Illinois	April, 1950	Korean War; polio scare
Graduate high school	June, 1957	Eisenhower is President; Little Rock confrontation
Graduate college	June, 1961	JFK is President; Peace Corps created
Get married	October, 1962	Cuban Missile Crisis
Sarah born	December, 1963	"I Have a Dream" speech; JFK killed
Julia born	February, 1968	Tet Offensive; MLK and RFK killed
May born	November, 1970	Kent State killings
Father dies	June, 1973	Watergate scandal; Roe v. Wade decision
Start new job	August, 1980	Mt. St. Helens erupts; Iran hostage crisis
First grandchild born	March, 1989	Cold War ends; Berlin Wall falls
Mother dies	April, 1991	Persian Gulf War
Second grandchild born	August, 1997	Princess Diana dies
Third grandchild born	September, 2001	World Trade Center attacked by terrorists
Retire	April, 2007	Virginia Tech massacre

BECOMING A TEENAGER

"When I was a boy of fourteen, my father was so ignorant I could hardly stand to have the old man around. But when I got to be twenty-one, I was astonished at how much the old man had learned in seven years." —Mark Twain

For most of us, adolescence is an exciting yet difficult time. No longer a child but not yet an adult, trapped in an awkward, transitional period of mental and physical change. What were your teenage years like, those years from age 13 to 18 or 19, or until you left home? Use the following questions to help you remember:

- What did you look like as a teenager? Describe yourself. How did your appearance change as you grew older?

- How were you like other teenagers? How were you different?

- Who were your best friends? How did you become friends with each other? Did any friendships last into adulthood, or even through to today?

- Did you learn how to drive? If so, who taught you? What was it like?

•◦ Who "showed you the ropes" early in life? And what "ropes" did you learn? Did you learn lessons the hard way, or did everything come easy to you?

•◦ Who or what most influenced you during your teenage years? How, and why?

•◦ Describe your high school. How large was it? What courses and extracurricular activities were offered? Which teachers do you remember most? What did you like about the school? Explain.

•◦ What did you do that you weren't supposed to do? Did you ever get into serious trouble? Was there ever a time when you insisted on doing something you felt to be important or right despite your parents' wishes?

•◦ How did you feel about becoming a man or woman? How did you learn the facts of life?

•◦ Did you participate in a religious ceremony or other event that marked a rite of passage toward adulthood?

•◦ What was the world like when you graduated from high school? What were some of your 18-year-old self's dreams?

•◦ Have you ever attended a high school reunion? If so, what was it like?

What were you considered when you were between the ages of 13 and 19? Were you a *teenager*, an *adolescent*, a *young person*, or still *one of the kids*? At what point were you considered a "grown-up"? Think about typical "rites of passage," such as being confirmed in a church or synagogue, getting to sit at the grown-ups' table for celebrations, receiving a driver's license, being eligible for military service, or getting married. Which of these apply to you?

Stories about becoming an adult and "learning the facts of life" can be fascinating to young relatives, who are accustomed to being bombarded with sexual information from a young age. Think about this as you write the story of your life, and make mention of it accordingly.

WRITING TIPS

After you have written four or five chapters, put them aside for a few weeks. Then go back and reread your work. First, you will almost certainly be pleased with what you have written. Second, you will be reminded of other incidents, episodes, and details that will need to be included.

As you go back and edit your writing, try to read it as though it were written about a complete stranger. Keep in mind the newspaper writer's questions: Who? What? When? Where? Why? How? Be sure to answer these questions for your readers. Also go a step further and include how you *felt* about the people, places, and events you describe.

READING SUGGESTIONS

•❖ *An American Childhood* by Annie Dillard—Dillard recounts growing up in a middle-class family in the Midwest in the 1950s.

IN THE WORDS OF REAL PEOPLE

Then came another crisis. I had stepped across the border from childhood to womanhood when I started to menstruate in January. Now in August—nothing! I was devastated. I knew from very limited instruction from my mother that this meant I was going to have a baby. I knew, vaguely, that a man had to figure into this situation, but I didn't know any men. I racked my brain to think this through and finally remembered that at the Saturday movie a month before, the knee of the man who sat beside me had touched mine. That was it! And I had no idea who he was, the father of my child. What would my mother say? I thought I would have to run away rather than bring disgrace on my family. Oh, I was upset; I couldn't even confide in my best friend, it was so disgraceful.

I kept my guilty secret until one night when I waited until my mother was in bed with the lights out. I crept into her darkened room to ask my embarrassing questions and to confess that I was to have a baby and knew why that was. It's a good thing that we were in the dark, for my poor mother must have had a terrible time trying not to laugh. As it was, she was overcome with a coughing fit while I waited to be banished from the family. When she finally could talk, she drew me into her arms and comforted me, telling me that sometimes there are irregularities in the menstrual cycle. I felt better but didn't really breathe a sigh of relief until the next month when I was back on schedule.

Marietta Hetherington Neumeister

I vividly remember one Saturday afternoon when I went to the movies with my best friend, Frances. There, we thought we were so grown up, enjoying the flick and smoking cigarettes.

All of a sudden Frances poked me in my arm with her elbow.

"What's your problem?" I asked her.

Very unexpectedly, my ear was enveloped in a vise-like grip. Looking up, I saw my mother, who had come to join us for the movie. Surprised and astonished, I choked on the smoke. She had caught me.

Not a word was spoken all the way home, nor was the grip on my ear released.

Benita Ackerman

After Lee Norell entered my life, all I could think about was him. I found out that he lived across the street from my cousin Jeanne. Needless to say, I found ways of spending a lot of time at Jeanne's house. Jeanne was 5 years older than I, and she didn't really want me around all that much. To her, I was the brat cousin. But time and tenacity paid off. Lee finally noticed me.

One late fall evening, Lee and I and a couple kids from our class walked about a mile from his house to Norwegian Hill, known also as "lover's lane". My innocence was obvious, yet I hankered for just one kiss. Then my life would be complete. Nothing like that happened. Instead we kicked fallen leaves and chased each other around trees. It was getting late, so we decided it was time to walk me home, since I lived the furthest distance away.

As we turned the corner and started down the alley toward my house, James and Alice were far ahead of us. It was a full moon night and had become colder than when we first started out. My nose was running, but I didn't want to sniff or use my finger or sleeve to take care of the problem. Lee was not to think of me as a slob. When we arrived near my house, Lee impishly pulled me into a shadow, where he kissed me. Hard. It was an endless kiss, like Rhett Butler and Scarlett O'Hara in that steamy scene just before he grabs her and runs up the stairs. I collapsed into the youthful passion of that moment. Then, suddenly, I got the giggles. Without disengaging my lips, I snorted. And that's when everything I had in my nose flew out onto his face. I was mortified and began apologizing profusely. But he, being a true gentleman just said, "Oh, that's all right," while wiping the mess off with his handkerchief.

Donna Davis, *Dancing in the Cactus Patch*

TEENAGE LIFE

"The old believe everything, the middle-aged suspect everything, the young know everything." —Oscar Wilde

The lives of teenagers change from generation to generation—yet, as the old adage goes, the more things change, the more they stay the same. Think about your life as a teenager: your interests, your hobbies, your ideals. What was life like then? Despite some insecurity, many people find experiences at this age to be the most cherished and the most memorable of their entire lives.

- Describe popular entertainment during your teenage years. Did you go to the movies, listen to the radio, or watch television? What dances were popular? What music? What did you and your friends do for fun?

- What were fashions like when you were a teenager? What about the hairstyles?

- Did you have any teenage idols or heroes? Who were they? What was your inspiration?

- Did you worry about money often? How did you earn money? What did you usually spend it on?

- What was the most embarrassing thing that happened to you as a teenager? The funniest? The loneliest time you experienced?

- How did you feel about members of the opposite sex? Did you go on dates? What did you do? Where did you go? Do you remember any date especially well? Why?

- What national and/or international events affected you—for example: the Depression, World War II, John F. Kennedy's assassination, the war in Vietnam, Tiananmen Square, or Hurricane Katrina?

- Were you involved in any popular movements or organizations? If so, what did you do with them?

Rarely are we so regularly embarrassed as when we're teenagers. When you recall those moments, your hands may be sweating and you breathe a bit shallowly and your face becomes flushed and it all comes flying back. Ah, some memories are best avoided!

However, it is a good idea to be honest in your writing, even though honesty about your teenage years might involve some "true confessions."

WRITING TIPS

A well-developed sense of humor keeps many people going through the difficult times of their lives. Yet too often, people become oh-so-serious whenever they pick up a pen to write. Remember to let your sense of humor shine through in your writing. You might also want to include jokes, cartoons, or other humorous material throughout your autobiography.

READING SUGGESTION

➥ *Angela's Ashes: A Memoir* by Frank McCourt—In his Pulitzer Prize-winning memoir, McCourt vividly describes his childhood in Ireland. He writes without bitterness—and often with humor—about growing up in extreme poverty with hunger, disease, and an irresponsible, alcoholic father.

IN THE WORDS OF REAL PEOPLE

Sometimes I would be allowed to go to a dance on Saturday night. I was a good dancer, often a favorite partner for several men. In those days we danced in the local community house in our town in Denmark. The rich boys would stand in one corner, the hired hands in another, the farmers' daughters in a third corner, and lastly, the hired girls in the fourth corner. We would have two or three musicians to play, usually an accordion and a fiddle or two. The dances were mostly square dances, polkas, and waltzes. As soon as the music started up, you would see the men make for their favorite dance partner, sometimes running to beat another guy to the girl. The men would bow to the girls. If she curtsied it meant yes, she would dance with him. If she didn't, he would try another. Often a complete dance would be finished without a single word spoken; the man would then offer you his arm and walk you back to where you had been standing.

The usual seating in the room was some benches along the walls, never more than for some of the rich girls and maybe a chair for the musicians. It was always a thrill to have several men wanting to dance with you. We didn't have any refreshments, except water from the pump, but there were always some men who went outside to drink beer or schnapps. They were not really welcome inside at the dance. We always had a bouncer to keep everybody in line. The one I remember best was Martin; he was a big burly man, a friend of everyone, but tough on any drunk. There was never any kissing or hugging going on in the hall, but flashing eyes and body language were strong. If a man was interested in you he would ask you to go for a walk during the intermission, but a nice girl would not go outside with a man. If she did she was not considered a nice girl. If you had a steady boyfriend, he would ask you sometime during the evening if he could take you home. We would all be on our bikes, and often the man would have several miles to ride back to the farm where he was working. Of course some of them would hope for a little more than a good night kiss when they came to the girl's place, and some of them got it, but generally it was, at most, some petting and kissing, at least in the crowd I ran with. I never remember being picked up or met at home until I was engaged to Hans. For the dances we met at the hall, always hoping this one or that one would ask you to dance, or ride home with you.

During the dance, a farmer's son would never dance with any of the hired girls. The same for the hired hands, who would never dream of dancing with the farmers' daughters. The rules were unspoken but strict. The men with a trade such as a clerk, a bricklayer, a carpenter, or such were in the in-between group, a step up from the hired farm hand but one step below the farmer's son. The teachers were held in high regard because of their knowledge.

As most of us worked on the farms and the farm hands only had cold water from the pump and a cold room in the barn to wash and change in, the odor in the dance hall would become very strong, as sweating bodies would emit their many mixed perfumes. I don't remember it bothering us at all; today I shudder to think what we all must have smelled like.

The floor in the hall was wooden planks. On dance night the floor would be sprinkled with soap flakes to make it slippery and easy to dance on. Later it would also be much easier to scrub. Many of us would wear wooden shoes, and at certain points in the dance, the men would really stomp hard and swing the girls high in the air, so by 2 a.m. the soap was worked completely into the planks. At one place the wooden floors were replaced with colored cement, which was a nice reddish brown. By the end of the evening we all had reddish brown clothes, faces, and hands . . .

If anybody today . . . had only half as good a time as we had in the 40s with wartime and no money, they would be lucky and as happy as we were, in many ways. We didn't have time to think about where "to find ourselves," or whom we should blame if we had a hard life. You stayed at your job and you took the knocks life dished out. We had very clear lines of what we could do or be, and most of us didn't stray.

Agnes Clausen, *The Track of the Wooden Shoes*

LEAVING HOME

"All adventures, especially into new territory, are scary." —*Sally Ride*

All of us—or almost all of us—eventually leave home, ready to become self-sufficient adults. How did you take your leave and enter the world of being grown up? Was it hard? Was it exciting? Did you go on an adventure? Did you move far away?

Some of the ironies of being human are enchanting to think about. We spend a great deal of thought and energy as children just waiting and wishing we were grown up. Then as adults we yearn to be young again!

⚬ At what point did you move away from home? Why and where did you go? What did you do? If you never moved, explain why.

- What were your dreams, goals, and ambitions as you set off into the world? Did you reject any family values, or even the family itself? Which family values did you keep with you?

- Record some of the difficulties you had in becoming an adult. When did you consider yourself an adult?

- If you attended college, tell about your college years. What did you study? What do you remember most? How did it affect the rest of your life?

- If you joined one of the military services, describe those years. What were your duties? What kind of effect did military service have upon you?

- What were some of your early jobs? How did you get those jobs? What kind of training prepared you? Which job was the most satisfying, and why?

- What were some of the best experiences you had with your newfound freedom? How did you feel, living away from home? Was it good to get out on your own? Was it frightening?

We each come of age in our own way. The birth of our adult personality comes slowly over a stretch of our teenage and young adult years. A fully realized person emerges from the seed pod of a young child. How did you do this? And how did you know when you had reached adulthood?

Some women left their growing-up homes to get married. The next chapter deals with that event specifically, so if you want to write about that, just jump ahead. There is also a specific set of questions in the next chapter about jobs and careers. If you entered the military right out of high school, describe that decision, your training, and your service. Leaving home is concerned with a moment of time: when you walked out of your growing-up home. It's an important moment, so give it the attention it deserves before you move on to the next chapter and write about your adult life.

WRITING TIPS

Has your curiosity ever been aroused by a television report, only to discover you aren't going to get any more details? The details, of course, are what make a story interesting!

As you write your memoirs, remember to give your readers plenty of information. Go over what you have written, and add more details. Then go back and add some more.

It may be tempting to write something like this: "Because of Vietnam, I got married too quickly." That sentence doesn't tell your readers much. You need to describe exactly how the situation affected you personally. Did you get married in a hurry because your husband was going overseas? Did you wear a navy blue suit instead of the white dress you had always dreamed about? How did you feel about having a small wedding—and then a husband who was an ocean away for perhaps several years? How did you cope? How did you feel? Adding details will bring your story to life.

READING SUGGESTIONS

➸ *It Was on Fire When I Lay Down on It* by Robert Fulghum— One essay in this book describes in amusing detail some of the "icky" things grown-ups end up doing, concluding with the observation that being an adult is dirty work.

Chapter 4
Remembering and Writing: Adult Life

ORGANIZING

*"The secret of all victory lies in the organization
of the non-obvious." —Marcus Aurelius*

As you begin writing about your adult years, you must make an organizational decision. To this point, you have been writing in a mostly chronological fashion. You have followed the events and feelings you experienced as a child up through young adulthood.

Now you may want to organize your writing differently. Below are four different ways to organize an autobiography. As you write about your adult years, you may want to take one of these approaches.

CHRONOLOGICAL APPROACH

The chronological approach is the easiest method to use when you begin an autobiography. Big changes occurred in your life between the ages of 5 and 15, and it is easy to recall memories in the order of occurrence. There is a big difference between being 5 years old and being 10 years old. However there is not much difference between being 32 and 37 or 58 and 63. Because memories of later years tend to run together, a chronological approach can become more difficult as you progress with your autobiography.

TOPICAL APPROACH

When writing about adult years, it often becomes easiest to write by topic. Instead of writing a yearly record of events, you may prefer to write chapters on different subjects, like marriage, raising children, jobs, or hobbies. Some writers have used a different individual as the focus of each chapter, calling the first chapter "Granny," another "Dad," a third "Martin," and so on.

TURNING POINTS OF LIFE

Certain writers enjoy writing their life stories from the perspective of looking back at significant turning points in their lives. They describe how different circumstances and choices helped determine the course of their lives and helped to shape them as individuals.

The "turning points" method is a psychologically sophisticated one, and difficult for some individuals to handle as an overall method of organization. However, all writers can readily handle the two assignments that use this approach: "Turning Points" (p. 143) and "Who Are You—Really?" (p. 152).

HISTORICAL PERSPECTIVE

Some people tell their life stories from a historical perspective. Many introduce each chapter with a brief summary of the cultural, political, and historical events of a particular period of time. Then they tell their own stories, describing how they were affected by history and how they contributed to the history of their time.

Most of you will include at least some information from a historical perspective in your autobiography. For example, few soldiers can fail to address the impact war had upon their lives, and neither can the wives and girlfriends they left behind. Activities like "Timeline" (p. 63) and "A Few Memorable Dates" (p. 134) will help you write from a historical perspective.

As you look over the questions in the exercises that follow, think about what method of organization makes the most sense to you.

VIPS

"I have always depended on the kindness of strangers."
—*Blanche DuBois in* A Streetcar Named Desire

Who are the VIPs in your life? VIPs are Very Important People. They are not "stars"—not your mother, spouse, mentor, or best friend—but people who are important nevertheless. They are people who have touched your life in some important way, if only briefly.

A Very Important Person could be a neighbor, a classmate, a national or local politician, or a chance acquaintance whose name you never even knew. It could be a pet, a character from a book, a movie star, a buddy in the service, a teacher—anyone who meant something to you in your lifetime, for whatever reason.

Remember that if all of the people in the entire world were listing their VIPs, you would probably be found on many lists. Each of us is certainly a VIP to many others, even though we may not realize it.

Take this opportunity to list 25–50 of the VIPs in your life, and write a short descriptive phrase about each person.

IN THE WORDS OF REAL PEOPLE

It's simple—I am afraid of flying. I'm not like John Madden and others who share this fear and never fly. I still fly. My fearfulness begins with just the thought of being on an airplane.

On one occasion, I boarded a plane in Las Vegas, heading home to Denver. We were nearly ready for takeoff when he entered the plane. He was one of the largest men I have ever seen. He was so tall that he had to duck his head to make it through the archway. He was a large Black man, not really obese, just very, very large in stature. After he placed his luggage in the compartment, he settled down into the seat by the window, next to mine.

When the plane began to taxi down the runway for takeoff, I took a deep breath and closed my eyes. The stranger spoke to me in the kindest, gentlest voice I have ever heard from a man, other than my own father, and said, "Are you afraid of flying?"

"Yes," I said in embarrassment.

"Do you believe?" he asked.

"Yes," I said. "I pray a lot before I get on the plane and always when I'm on the plane, too."

"Look out there—that beautiful sky, those puffy white clouds—it's like a little piece of Heaven. You are close to God. He will cradle this plane in his hands and keep us safe. He will guide us through the air safely and then gently set us down on the earth at the end of our flight. Trust him." I looked into this stranger's eyes and never have I felt engulfed with more peacefulness. His eyes were so kind. I felt protected.

He introduced himself. "My name is Hugh. My mother wasn't a very educated woman, and I truly believe she must have been trying to spell Huge!"

During the flight, Hugh and I talked and talked about anything and everything, mostly about families and dreams. "Well, if I could live out my dream, it would be to sit along a river in the mountains of Colorado and fish," he told me.

"Oh!" I exclaimed. "That can come true. My husband and I have a cabin in the mountains, right along the river. We would be thrilled if you and your wife would come and be our guests someday."

I wrote our name, phone number, and address and told him to call if he was ever back in Colorado and had time to share with us. "I would love that," he said and wrote everything down.

Never has a flight seemed so short, and never have I flown before or since with such a feeling of total security. As our flight was nearing an end, Hugh looked at me and said,

"No one has ever been as nice to me as you have been on this flight. I am so thankful that it was you I was to sit by. You needn't be afraid anymore, I will be with you on all your flights from now on—in spirit, I mean, of course."

When I sent a Christmas card to Hugh and his wife, the card came back—"no such address." I quickly tried to call him and heard: "The number you have dialed is not in service at this time." When I checked with directory assistance, the operator said, "I'm sorry. There is no Hugh McKinnon listed in the Michigan area, and Michigan has no prefix matching the one you have given me."

Who was he? In my heart, I know God sent a real live angel to share that flight with me and help me through my fear. Angels do truly come in all sizes and all colors, but none more beautiful to me than this very large Black man who called himself Hugh McKinnon.

Lorene Putnam

On one of my Saturday trips to downtown Minneapolis to ride the very first escalator in town, at Dayton's department store, I was caught impulsively shoplifting a package of gum at Woolworth's 5- and 10-cent store. I was ushered into a dimly lit basement room with two chairs and a table. I was told to wait for the store detective to come in and interrogate me. The package of Dentyne gum lay in the middle of the table as a reminder of my crime.

Finally the door opened, and a stern and factual man took his place in a chair at the table. I was not asked to sit down. I just stood there shaking. He offered me two alternatives of punishment. Number one was that he would notify my dad and let him deal with me appropriately. Number two was that for the next three Saturdays, I would walk or run to the downtown Woolworth's store. I was not to hitchhike or take the street car for the 5-mile trip. I would go directly to the Woolworth office and ask for him. I was to look him directly in the eyes and on my word of honor profess that I had not stolen anything all week and that I had made a terrible mistake in stealing the Dentyne gum. Needless to say, I accepted the second option.

After my third probation session, he shook my hand and led me to the Dentyne gum display that was so tempting to me 3 weeks earlier. He reached into the pile of gum and picked out a package of gum and handed it to me. I was reluctant to accept it, but the clerk behind the counter reassured me that it was okay. The detective shook my hand again and in so doing slipped a street car token into my hand so that I could ride the street car 5 miles to my home. We never saw each other again, but the lesson of sternness yet compassion has lived with me all of these years. My life as a shoplifter was short-lived.

Bob Jackson

ROMANCE, LOVE, AND MARRIAGE

"Marriage is a great institution, but I'm not ready for an institution, yet." —Mae West

There is a reason why romantic love remains such a popular theme in books and movies: it is a subject that is important to all of us. How have romance, love, and/or marriage affected you over the years?

Writing about feelings is hard for people who were brought up in a time when we didn't "let it all hang out" or "tell it like it is." Many of us grew up hearing that "boys don't cry" and "ladies don't express anger." Sharing feelings is difficult as it makes us vulnerable to one another. It is risky—but so is buying a house, getting married, having children, or changing jobs. Taking risks often leads to the greatest rewards in life. Think about how wonderful it would be if you knew what your grandparents felt about the events in their lives. You can give that gift of wonder to your grandchildren and future generations. Take the risk!

• What family stories do you know about love and romance? For example, do you know how your parents or grandparents met? Are there family stories about lost love, elopements, or unusual courtships?

- ⮞ Describe your first love. How old were you? Who was the object of your love? How did things work out?

- ⮞ Have you had important romances that did not end in marriage? Describe them.

If you have ever been married, write about your marriage (or marriages). Here are a few questions:

1. How did you and your spouse meet? How old were you? What were the qualities and characteristics that attracted you to one another? How did you know you were in love?

2. Describe your wedding. What did you wear? Did you follow any family traditions? Did you go on a honeymoon?

3. Describe your adjustments to married life. What was easy? What was difficult? Were there any surprises? How did you and your spouse resolve differences?

4. What was the best—and the worst—thing about being married that first year?

5. Have you ever been divorced? If so, how did the divorce affect you? How did you cope with the changes that resulted?

WRITING TIPS

When writing about marriage, you have the wonderful opportunity to give your opinions in a nonjudgmental and very personal way, without preaching. Instead of writing about what young people *should* do, you might write about what *you* did when the road toward marital bliss got bumpy. Be honest. If, for example, you sometimes wished divorce had been more acceptable when you were young, write about your thoughts and feelings at the time. Also, you might write about what you observed in the marriages of your parents, grandparents, and other relatives and friends.

It is important to include stories of your spouse's growing-up years, to establish who he or she was before you entered the scene. So flesh this person out a bit—if he or she is alive, ask for help. If you are a widow or widower, you must tell the story! Here are some questions to consider:

- When and where was your spouse born and raised?

- What kind of family was he or she raised in? Were there siblings? Who were they? Where did she or he come in the birth order? Did this matter?

- Was your spouse's family well off financially or did they struggle?

- Describe your spouse's mother and father, reminding your readers that this is your perspective. Did you get along with your spouse's family?

- Did your spouse partake in any notable adventures before meeting you? Relate some of the life experiences that shaped him or her into the person you eventually married.

READING SUGGESTIONS

- "Among Other Thoughts on Our Wedding Anniversary," from *How Did I Get to Be 40 . . . & Other Atrocities* by Judith Viorst— In this lighthearted poem about marriage, Viorst lists all the little things that have gone wrong over the years—and that she has been happy to blame on her husband.

- *Gift From the Sea* by Anne Morrow Lindbergh—Lindbergh's reflections on being a woman, wife, and mother include the observation that few of the saints have been married women. She writes that "It has to do primarily with distractions"—distractions like feeding and educating children, running a house, and dealing with human relationships.

IN THE WORDS OF REAL PEOPLE

We met at the dance, and neither of us had eyes for anybody else. I still see Hans as he looked that night. Due to the war, we were all unable to buy any kind of clothes, so we all had to make do with what we could scrounge anywhere. Hans looked very nice in a dark suit, but underneath it he had a maroon shirt with a narrow white stripe. Over a period of time the collar had completely worn out, so his mom had hemmed it neatly around the neck. Above it he wore a cardboard collar, and because of the stiffness of the cardboard, he had been unable to get on a normal tie. He had borrowed his dad's black funeral tie; it was pre-knotted and had an elastic band that could be tucked up into the cardboard collar. He later told me his dad had used a kitchen knife to get this feat accomplished.

We danced every dance. There was just one thing wrong, and that was the heavy way Hans perspired. As the evening wore on, the collar started to disintegrate. By the end of the dance all that was left around his neck was the black elastic band from the tie. His suit had shrunk, the pants only reaching to the ankles. He had taken the jacket off during all the hard work of the waltzes and polkas, so the maroon shirt was now covered by shreds of paper. It was absolutely hilarious, but all my girlfriend Herdis could see was a man in a very dilapidated state, and when I told her I had agreed to his walking me home, Herdis said, "You are not letting that man take you home," with every sign of distaste on her face. I did, however, do as I wanted, and that became the start of almost 40 years of bliss with Hans.

Agnes Clausen, *The Track of the Wooden Shoes*

During the gasoline shortage in the 1970s, Fridays were special days for Joe and me. We grocery shopped in Greeley, did a host of errands we'd saved up, had dinner at a nice restaurant, and went to a movie. The evenings were topped off with a Baskin Robbins ice cream cone.

We were happy—we loved one another and respected one another's opinions. As Joe said, "We proved that a conservative male chauvinistic Republican and a liberal, feminist Democrat can get along—if they don't talk politics!" I do think I persuaded him to be a bit more liberal about some issues, though, and I have to admit that being a capitalist (in a small way) isn't all bad. He taught me some useful facts about investments and investing. As a widow, those lessons have helped me manage my income better than I might have.

Hazel Chick, Memory Is the Haunting of the Heart

The day after we arrived at our Albuquerque apartment, Bob went back to work, and the first night we had bacon and eggs for dinner. The next morning when I woke up, it dawned on me for the first time that I didn't know how to cook. We had received seven cookbooks for wedding presents, but they were all being shipped from Detroit. I learned to cook in a hurry.

Sue Schulze, No Fun Like Work

Art and I were married on August 4, 1927, in my parents' home. His father attended the wedding, but his mother did not. She felt her son was marrying below his station. But as the years went by, she mellowed and upon her death left me an electric lawn mower.

Uba Stanley, Uba Stanley's Sojourn on This Planet Earth

SERIOUS WRITERS

"Discipline is the bridge between goals and accomplishment." —Jim Rohn

People often have misconceptions about writers. They see writers as people sitting around waiting for inspiration to hit. In reality, most serious writers find discipline more important than inspiration. They view writing as hard work—work they enjoy, but work nonetheless. Because their work is difficult, writers do whatever it takes to help them get their job done.

Ernest Hemingway had to have dozens of perfectly sharpened pencils nearby when he wrote. John Steinbeck needed round pencils at the ready, complaining that a hexagonal pencil cut his fingers after a long day. Vladimir Nabokov had to have relatively soft pencils capped with good erasers. Virginia Woolf and Lewis Carroll wrote standing up, while Truman Capote and Mark Twain wrote lying down.

Many writers today take their laptops to coffee shops or other locations to write. Some use tablets and smartphones to help organize their ideas. Others enter online writing contests like National Novel Writing Month (NaNoWriMo, http://www.nanowrimo.org) as motivation to finish their work.

As you write your autobiography, set goals for yourself. Writer Julia Cameron, author of *The Artist's Way* suggested "Set small and gentle goals, and meet them." Another contemporary author, Anne Lamott, who wrote *Bird by Bird*, suggested writing "an inch at a time," and giving yourself permission to write terrible first drafts, just to get the process started.

The important thing is to let go of the notion of perfection and to get words down on paper. You can edit later.

Do whatever works for you to encourage yourself to make a commitment to writing.

WRITING ABOUT YOUR CHILDREN

"It takes a village to raise a child." —Proverb

Before you begin the sections on "Being a Parent" and "Family Life," be aware that there are many approaches to writing about children. It's a good idea to think about how you will approach the subject of being a parent before you begin.

Some people find it easy to write about their sons and daughters. In fact, they find it so easy that they become bogged down in the details of their children's lives and never really move forward. Be careful that you don't become "stuck" as you write about your children. You have a lot more of your own life to write about.

On the other hand, many people find it terribly difficult to write about their sons and daughters. They worry about what their children will think, knowing that children can be very critical judges, especially when the subject is themselves. Writers may find it difficult to write about a child who has been a disappointment, who has had an unhappy life, or who has died prematurely. Or they may find it difficult to write because they feel they have failed as a parent. If, for whatever reason, you find it difficult to write about your children (or a particular child), don't feel that you have to address the subject all at once. Try writing just a bit, knowing that you can always come back to the subject later. When the time is right, the words will come.

It is important to be honest when writing about your children. However, do be aware of balance. Don't write two pages about one child and only two sentences about another. No matter how old children are, they still want to be special in the eyes of their parents.

Many people choose not to write a section about each of their children as individuals. Instead, they write about parenthood and family life in general, relating incidents about individual children only as they come up in the writers' life stories. They have the philosophy that their autobiography is the story of their life, not their children's lives. If you take this approach, it will serve you well to pay special attention to the final question in the following section: *How has each child added to your life?*

If you have never had children, you may choose to skip right to "The Working World" (p. 96). Or you may instead want to write about the children who have been important in your life: perhaps nieces and nephews, stepchildren, or the children of close friends. How have these children been important to you? How have they affected your life? You may also want to write about why you never had children. Was it a conscious choice? Was it for some reason not possible? How do you feel now about not having children? What was the impact of not having children on your life?

BEING A PARENT

"Babies are necessary to grown-ups. A new baby is like the beginning of all things—wonder, hope, a dream of possibilities." —Eda LeShan

Being a parent is one of the most difficult, yet most rewarding, jobs in the world. If you have been a parent, then you know just how true that can be. Life changes dramatically once you become a parent, and it never returns to the way it was before. Tell about the role parenthood has played in your life, and all of the changes that took place once you stepped into that role.

- Who are your children? List their full names and dates of birth. How did you choose their names? What circumstances where they born into?

- How are you different as a parent from your own parents? How are you the same?

- What, to you, is most frightening about parenthood?

- Did you and your spouse generally agree about how to raise your children? What did you agree on? What did you disagree about?

- What have been some of your proudest or most rewarding moments as a parent? What happened? Who was involved?

- How did you handle the less pleasant parts of raising children—sibling rivalry, bickering, teenage rebellion?

- How were your children different from each other when they were small? How were they alike? Did you treat them the same or differently? How and why?

- Assess yourself as a parent. What would you do the same, if you had it to do all over again? What would you do differently? What do you hope your children have learned from you?

➥ Describe each of your children. Relate some favorite stories about each. How has each child added to your life?

READING SUGGESTIONS

➥ "Charles," from *Life Among the Savages* by Shirley Jackson— This classic tale provides a mother's humorous account of her son's experiences in kindergarten.

IN THE WORDS OF REAL PEOPLE

When Cleone showed signs that it was time for the baby to be delivered, we had a problem. They moved her to a cart and wheeled her into the hall, where a nurse said, "Take her back in. The red-haired lady is supposed to be next. The order of patients has already been arranged!" I did not believe what I heard and protested to our nurse, who said, "She is my floor superior; we must wait." Cleone told me, "Honey, the baby IS COMING!" I patted her shoulder and said, "It's okay. Just go ahead and have the baby on the cart, here in the hall. Hold my hand . . . and PUSH!" I spoke LOUDLY so that the nurse could hear what we planned to do, and she went trotting down the hall. Soon the red-haired woman came wheeling back out, and Cleone was wheeled in. I was sent to the waiting room.

What they didn't know, and what Cleone didn't know, was that the seat in that waiting room was right in front of an upper air duct. That duct was like an earphone; I could hear EVERY word from the delivery room. Throughout the delivery, I sweated like a furnace-room worker, hanging on every groan and sharp-voiced urging of Dr. Sullivan. I knew when Cleone hurt, and I knew why. I heard a play-by-play delivery of the birth of our son, even though I wasn't allowed in the delivery room.

Robert Vail, *Dew on a Leaf*

When our daughters ranged in age from thirteen down to three, my husband decided it was time to take them out

West. On the way to a friend's abandoned homestead in the Colorado hills, we stopped in Cheyenne to take in the Frontier Days Rodeo and to outfit the girls with cowboy hats and boots.

From then on 3-year-old Cornelia was a cowboy. When I told her that it was bedtime, she said that cowboys didn't go to bed that early. When I urged her to eat her vegetables, she said that cowboys only ate meat.

When we took our first horseback ride into the hills, Cornelia had to ride in front of me in my saddle. It was evidently too close a fit because, although she said not a word, after an hour she took my hand and inserted it between her stomach and the saddlehorn. It was a hot day, and it never occurred to the only real cowboy in the group that we might be getting tired and thirsty. Finally Cornelia twisted around, looked up at me with a sad little face and said, "Let's go home. I aren't a cowboy."

Barbara Anne Green, *Journals*

According to our outline for writing, this is where I'm supposed to assess myself as a parent. I shouldn't have cut Robb's hair in a flat top when he was in high school and wanted a new style. I shouldn't have made Lynn bundle up and go out in the cold and stay until he could come in and not be so obnoxious. I should have waited a couple of years to go to work because Gary really didn't like coming home from school without me being there for him. Maybe I shouldn't have turned around to the backseat and slapped Gwyn when we were on our way to church and she asked, "Why the hell do I have to go?" She wanted to do something else that day. But as long as I didn't do something to mark them for life, I must have been an average parent. I know I tried to raise them to know right from wrong, to be independent and well adjusted. I wanted them to be God-loving children who would, as adults, be an asset to their family, community and country. I should have done some things I didn't and shouldn't have done some things I did, but I tried hard and was very confident I was a good parent.

Mary Casseday, *Pathways*

I have three children, two boys and a girl. I thought it would be interesting to know the definition of *children*, so where does one go but to the dictionary. After finding *chili, chili con carne, chili rellenos,* I was ready for lunch. Okay, back to the children. The dictionary says to "see *child.*" *Child* said it's a noun. I knew that, but it's also a swelling up, womb, fetus, offspring, an infant baby, an unborn offspring, and on and on. I also came upon the word *childing,* the bearing of newer blossoms around an older blossom. I liked the picture of me as the gorgeous passion flower blossom of my youth surrounded by three of the most delicate and promising of gently opening buds.

Joan Milne, *And So It Was*

FAMILY LIFE

"There is little less trouble in governing a private family than a whole kingdom." —Michel de Montaigne

Family life is one of the strong "glues" of our society, yet every family is different from every other family. Describe yours. In what ways do you think your family is typical? How is it unique? Use the following questions to guide you as you write about your kin:

- ❧ What kind of family environment have you tried to create? Have you been successful?

- ❧ What makes your family special? Do you have special family words, sayings, or jokes?

- ❧ What are the rules in your family?

- ❧ Describe the most memorable trip your family has taken together. Why is it memorable?

- ❧ Tell some family stories and describe your adventures, embarrassing moments, and humorous episodes.

- ❧ Have pets been a part of your family? If so, tell their stories.

❧ What outside events have affected your family? Did a crisis or tragedy of some kind change the course of your lives? Did unforeseen circumstances like a financial windfall cause good fortune or special problems?

READING SUGGESTIONS

❧ *The Thirteenth Tale* by Diane Setterfield—This novel includes a breathtaking passage about how important it is to write memories down in order to keep people from disappearing forever.

A HOUSE BECOMES A HOME

"Home is the place where, when you have to go there, they have to take you in." —Robert Frost

It merits repeating that place is an important factor in who we are and who we become. Upon leaving your growing-up home, where did you find yourself living? In a house? A duplex? An apartment? Did you move often before settling down? Talk about your living space—or spaces—and how your home played into the lives of you and your family.

❧ What was the home you spent your early adult years in like? Describe it. Was it a house? With one or two stories? With a basement or an attic? Did you enter through the front door? Did it have a garage and a yard? A porch, a balcony, or a patio? Maybe a pool—or none of these things?

❧ What was the view like from your windows?

❧ What room did your family relax in? What would you typically do?

❧ Did you eat as a family for all meals? At the kitchen or dining room table, or maybe on trays, in front of the TV?

- How many bathrooms did you have? Was there a long line-up in the morning? Did you often run out of hot water?

- What is the quirkiest aspect of the home in which you raised your family?

- Did the kids hang out in their bedrooms, or all together? Did they keep their rooms tidy?

- What were the rules of the house (e.g., those dealing with phone calls, laundry, shoes inside, curfew, cleaning)?

- Where did you put the mail? Where did the kids drop their schoolwork and books? How about your coats—in the closet, or on the backs of chairs? Were you strict about this sort of thing?

- In your mind's eye, travel through your home—or homes, if you often moved—and write a story about each room. Which was your favorite? Why?

- When the children moved out, did the house feel like a different place? Describe how the atmosphere changed.

- Describe your dwelling on the day you moved in. What was it like then, and how is it now? If you've moved, tell how it looked (and how you felt) on the day you moved out.

READING SUGGESTIONS

- *A Family Place* by Charles Gaines—Gaines writes about building a summer cabin and rebuilding a family. It is a good reminder of the role place plays in the lives of individuals and families.

GETTING UNSTUCK

"Writer's block is for people who have the luxury of time." —Jodi Picoult

All writers sometimes get stuck. With autobiographical writing, it is important to look at *why* you are stuck.

Perhaps you just need a break. Sometimes your mind needs time to rest, to process, to mull over things. If so, put your autobiography on the "back burner" for a short time and come back to it later.

Perhaps you are having difficulty because you care too much about your audience's reaction. If this is the case, decide to get the truth as you see it down on paper, for now. Later you can edit and take out anything that you think is inappropriate or that might hurt someone.

Perhaps you are stuck because part of your past is very painful. If you were abused as a child, suffered betrayal by a spouse, or lost a child, it may seem impossible to write through your tears or anger or deep sadness. If so, tiptoe around the hurt or rage for a while. Move to a happier period of your life, and write about that. Eventually you will find yourself ready to write about painful times.

Sometimes people are stuck simply because they can't remember certain periods in their lives. If this happens to you, try taking yourself back to the period in your life you can't remember. Imagine yourself in a place from that time, perhaps school, home, downtown, or at dinner with a group of friends. Using your mind's eye, look at what you see. What do you hear? What do you smell? Taste? Feel? Memories are made using our five senses. If you work on invoking the senses, many memories are likely to come to mind. Another idea is to check with a friend, sibling, cousin, or anyone else who might help you remember events from a certain time in your life.

Remember that all authors sometimes find themselves getting stuck. Irving Stone once said, "When I have trouble writing, I step outside my studio into the garden and pull weeds until my mind clears—I find weeding to be the best therapy there is for writer's block." If you really can't write, walk away and do something else for a while. Come back later and try again.

THE WORKING WORLD

"I believe in the dignity of labor, whether with head or hand; that the world owes every man an opportunity to make a living." —John D. Rockefeller, Jr.

Work is an important part of all of our lives, whether that work is in the home or outside of the home. As with school as a child, time at the workplace takes up a significant chunk of everyday life. Write about the hours of each week that you have spent at your job. Have you held many different positions in a variety of fields, or were you steadily employed in a single career? Are you still employed now? Take this opportunity to talk about all of the hard work you've done—you've earned it!

- What jobs or careers have you had during your lifetime? Remember, being a homemaker counts!

- Would you choose other ways to make a living if you were to start all over again? Why or why not? What career choices were available to you?

- What personal qualities were helpful to you in your work?

Jobs and careers vary widely. To help you describe your work, whether inside or outside the home, take a look at the questions below:

- What was the hardest part of your job? The easiest?

- How do you feel about your work?

- What gave you the most pride and pleasure in your work?

- What was a typical day like?

- What equipment did you use on the job? Be sure to describe how the tools of your trade (including those for homemaking) were used, and how they have changed.

- What were your on-the-job worries and responsibilities?

- How did you feel about working for someone else? Or were you in charge?

- Did you ever make any wonderfully funny mistakes?

- Tell about the dangers of your work.

- What did you like best about your work? What did you like least?

- What surprised you about your work?

- Did you have a mentor at the workplace, or did you often "go it alone?"

- Did you ever lose your job? Did you ever experience a long period of unemployment? How did that feel? What did you do?

- Did your work define your identity, or do you think other terms or activities have better defined you? Has this perception changed over the years?

READING SUGGESTIONS

- *Working: People Talk About What They Do All Day and How They Feel About What They Do* by Studs Terkel—Terkel interviewed a wide variety of men and women working in the Chicago area in the 1970s. He compiled their stories into a fascinating history of jobs and careers.

IN THE WORDS OF REAL PEOPLE

After we were married, I decided to find a job where I could work Monday through Friday and have the weekends off. I was thankful then that I had taken typing and bookkeeping in high school. One of the few jobs you could find that fit these specifications was to be a secretary. I had no experience working this type job, but saw an opening in the want ad section of the *Tribune* that a bean company needed a secretary. I told myself I could do it. At this time of my life, I figured I could do anything I wanted to do if I wanted it badly enough, and I wanted this job. When I applied for it, I told him the truth and smiled a lot. I must have done something right, for when the interview was over, I had the job.

It was a fun job. My boss was like a farmer wearing a tie, and his wife was the head secretary bookkeeper. They were easy to work with and fun, too. Part of my job was cutting foot-square pieces of outing flannel and placing it on mesh wire with a wooden frame. This shelf would hold six strips long and two wide of flannel. When farmers would bring in their pinto beans, a worker in the warehouse would bring me a little sackful, and I would put one hundred beans, ten across and ten down, on each square of material, along with the farmer's name, dampen them a little and put the rack in an incubator for so many days to see how many would sprout. If a high enough percentage sprouted, they would be sold for seed beans. Otherwise they went for consumption. It was fun doing this and marking their charts. Besides, it gave me something to take me from my desk. It is funny the things that make an impression on you. This time it was my boss's wife. She was such a nice person, and was not heavy at all, but had very broad hips. Everyone said it was because she sat at that chair too many years. So I was glad to be able to get out of mine and do some walking and standing.

Mary Casseday, *Pathways*

Married women were not allowed to have full-time contracts to teach in Pueblo, CO, so I taught various things part-time, like boys' basketball, study hall, and a night class for women to exercise. I remember so well looking at obese women lying on the floor doing the bicycle exercise, and I thought, "I'll never allow myself to get like that."

I'm sure that the Lord lets us live just long enough to do everything we are so sure we will never do.

Uba Stanley, *Uba Stanley's Sojourn on This Planet Earth*

During the 10 years we lived full-time on the farm (1954–1964), I—like most farm wives—was the person to make trips to town for emergency repairs, act as mechanic's helper and occasional tractor or truck driver and assist in moving machinery from one field to another. In the region where we farmed, wheat harvest time was an especially hectic phase of the farming season, with extended working hours, additional workers to feed, extra trips to town for one reason or another, and a general sense of urgency to get the crop in the bin before a hailstorm would ruin it. The housewife along with the harvesters wearied of suppers at 9 o'clock at night and, worse, washing supper dishes at 10 o'clock and making any preliminary preparations for the next day's meals. And yet there was always a great sense of satisfaction and relief when this brief but hectic operation was concluded—especially if the harvest had been bountiful.

I still reflect on those years as a farm homemaker as being generally very happy and satisfying. Though sometimes frustrated with structural limitations of the old farmhouse and with limited financial resources, I responded with energy and imagination to the challenge of creating a home there, as well as a family.

Marge Curtiss

I did find a job just outside Lake Charles. It lasted half a day. I should explain.

The job was with an oil field construction company and consisted of lifting 2 X 12 boards out of the mud and loading them on a truck or trailer. These boards had formed a mat for an oil rig that had recently been dismantled.

After struggling in the hot sun—and getting one heck of a sunburn—from early morning until about noon, I lifted one of the mud-soaked boards. Wrapped around it was a copperhead snake just above my head as I carried the board to the truck. When I spotted the snake coiled around the board just inches from my head, I got rid of it fast and kept on walking, right out of a job. I never looked back.

Carroll Arnold, *Nothin's Easy*

SECRETS

"If you cannot get rid of the family skeleton, you may as well make it dance." —George Bernard Shaw

 Everyone knows the old saying "What you don't know won't hurt you." However, a family's hidden issues can have long-lasting effects, even through future generations. Incest, spousal abuse, child abuse, alcoholism, teenage pregnancy, and depression all tend to reappear in families, generation after generation. In fact, some psychologists believe that families who don't acknowledge and deal with their inner problems are doomed to repeat them.

For example, many men (and now women) were often advised by officers, ministers, priests, and rabbis upon discharge from military service not to share with their families or loved ones the horrors they experienced in war. The fear was that their families would view the newly discharged warriors as monster. And so the men who served in World War II, Korea, Vietnam, and, lately, countries in the Middle East often keep those memories buried deep inside them. Only now are many survivors of these wars telling their stories and creating understanding within their families.

Understanding can never come too late. By getting them out in the open, the airing of family secrets can make a profound—and positive—impact on the lives of your children and grandchildren.

- Are there any family secrets you have discovered that you wish you had known about much earlier? Explain.

- Are there any misconceptions or misunderstandings that have persisted between you and another person over the years? Was information hidden from someone?

- Are there any mysteries in your life that you wonder about or mysteries that have never been cleared up? Do you think your life would be different if you knew the truth?

- Are there any members of your family from whom you have tried to conceal certain truths? Why? Are there any who have tried to conceal truths from you?

- Is there anything people believe about you that is incorrect?

- Are there any secrets you would like to share with your children and grandchildren?

- Are there things you always wanted to say, things you wished you'd said, or things you wish you had not said or done?

READING SUGGESTIONS

- *In My Mother's House: A Memoir* by Kim Chernin—Chernin tells the story of her Russian Jewish mother, Rose Chernin, a Communist activist. She writes about working with her mother on the book, sharing secrets, and becoming, in the process, much closer to her.

ACROSS THE GENERATIONS

"I don't know who my grandfather was; I am much more concerned to know what his grandson will be." —Abraham Lincoln

You are a very important link in your family, a link between five or six generations. You have known your parents, your grandparents, and possibly your great-grandparents. You will know your children, grandchildren, and possibly great-grandchildren. You may have siblings, aunts and uncles, nieces and nephews. You are in a position to share important observations about your family, across the generations. Think about your family—your whole family—as you consider the following questions:

- Are there any physical characteristics, personality traits, or talents that run in your family? Perhaps red hair, stubbornness, or a talent for singing? Explain what you have observed about family traits over the years.

- What is the greatest nonmaterial gift your parents and/or grandparents have given you? What would be the greatest gift the children in your life could give you, or have already given you? What do you hope you have given them?

- Has any item been passed down from generation to generation in your family—perhaps a shawl, a quilt, a piece of jewelry, a watch fob, or a gun? Does it have a story?

- What characteristics or behaviors have you seen repeated in your family—for example, early marriage, alcoholism, academic careers, or having large families? Why do you think these patterns persist?

- Imagine that you could put a message into a time capsule to your family members to read or listen to 25 years from now. What would you say?

WRITING TIPS

Make a schematic like the one that follows, inserting the names of your family members in each heart. Think about how well the youngest members know about the lives of the oldest members. You are the only person who can connect the two ends of the spectrum; you have a moral obligation to introduce your great-grandmother to your great-grandson. If you do not make the connection, who will?

There is more to genealogy than names and dates. Think about how you can shed light into the true essence of the people inside each of these hearts and others in your family.

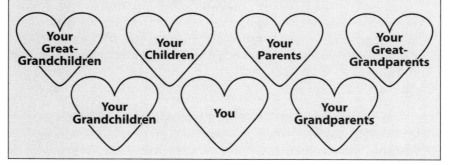

READING SUGGESTION

◆◇ *Pride of Family: Four Generations of American Women of Color* by Carole Ione—In this memoir, Ione writes about her mother's life, her grandmother's life, and the remarkable life of her great-grandmother, whose experiences were preserved in journals from after the Civil War. Ione discovers that the "spirits of all the women in my family past and present came to reside with me."

IN THE WORDS OF REAL PEOPLE

I can report that on both sides of my family, people were generally optimistic, cheerful, possessed of a good sense of humor, lifelong learners, concerned about the world around them in all of its various manifestations, hard workers, creative, effective problem solvers, caring for those less fortunate, and hospitable.

From what I have learned, members of my father's family were naturally possessed of good "people skills," that is, they were especially effective in dealing with people, particularly people who were irritated and disagreeable. They were capable of inspiring others to reach new heights in their own lives.

There have been many people with musical skills on both sides of my family. However, members of my mother's family probably developed those skills more highly through concentrated studies in that field. Family members have used those skills to entertain, to console, to inspire the communities in which they lived, and, in some instances, communities around the nation.

Members of both ancestral families have exhibited a creditable display of artistic talent, which continues into my children's generation. My father's sister, Alice, was a teacher of art in the schools of Boston. My mother and especially her sister, Frances, both studied art as young women. Frances continued to paint, especially in her years after age 60.

My ancestral families had many members who could be termed "joiners." That is, they participated fully in the life of the communities where they lived—joining churches, including choirs and other groups within the congregation, belonging to lodges, women's clubs, service organizations such as Lions and Rotary, card clubs, and political party organizations.

Marge Curtiss

One day my Great Aunt Maude Carlton told me that there were some family spoons, with a fancy 'M' engraved on the tip of the handle, which she and Grandma wanted me to have when I married. Of course, this made no impression on me at the time, and I forgot all about it.

But at my wedding reception, Aunt Maude, now very arthritic and in a wheelchair, pulled me down so she could speak in my ear. "Joe, you remember those spoons with the 'M' on them?" I did remember them, although it was the first time I'd thought of them since I was fourteen. "Yes," I said, expecting her to produce the package right then and there.

But no. Aunt Maude said, "Well, you're in the service now, and sooner or later you'll have to go overseas. And you might not come back. We all hope you do, of course, but you might not. So I've decided to keep them until you come back, if you do come back, and then I'll give them to you. If I were to give them to you now and you didn't come back (There! She'd said it again!), then they'd be in Lila's hands and out of the family, wouldn't they?" I had to admit that was a distinct possibility.

But the bad part of all this is that while I was away in the war, Aunt Maude passed away. She must have taken the spoons with her, for nobody has ever heard what became of them. I just may ask her someday Over There whatever became of them. Most people say that you can't take it with you. But a great planner like Aunt Maude may have discovered some way to do it . . . and she may be willing to give the spoons to us when we all meet over in Heaven. But if Lila goes first and I come after, I'll bet she'll have to wait until I get there for delivery of the goods in question. We certainly wouldn't want to let them get out of the family!

Joseph Wilson Mefford, Jr., *My Story, My Song*

The Sadler siblings shared an exuberant family spirit. Unlike my dour father's family, my mother's family was boisterous and entertaining. Several had musical inclinations that would spontaneously erupt any time they got together. They were as unruly as the Marx brothers, exhibiting high-spirited buffoonery comparable to the antics created by Harpo, Zeppo, Chico, and Groucho in any one of their Hollywood movies. The Sadlers would put on funny hats, and strange combinations of clothes, sing songs to a rhythm accompaniment of someone beating thimbles against a washboard. If there was a piano, one of them would beat out the melody while the other rolled a grapefruit back and forth over the bass keys, making a sound like a cacophonous drum. Ila sustained the tune with her tenor ukulele. And, most always, their hilarity ended far into the night, after plenty of drinks and something to eat.

My maternal grandmother gave her daughters three-lettered "power" names: Eva, Mae, Fae, Ora, and Ila. But her two sons were named, ordinarily enough, Harry and Donald. All of the children were brilliant and sensuously good-looking. Eva and Ora were destined to marry many times. Ora's husbands were usually younger than herself, and she married for the fifth time at age 82. Eva had only four trips to the altar before she died. And the strange thing is this: Both were married to their first husbands for 25 years. When they began making up for lost time, their brother Harry aptly nicknamed them "the poor man's Gabors."

Donna Davis, *Dancing in the Cactus Patch*

ILLUSTRATING YOUR STORY

"Even if you can't draw, do a little doodle or rip an illustration from a magazine—these visuals will help bring your idea to life." —John Emmerling

It is true that a picture is often worth a thousand words. Consider illustrating the fads and fashions of your youth with a collage. Using old books, catalogues, or other sources, photocopy pictures and drawings of anything "old-fashioned" that applies to your life. Cut up the individual photocopies and arrange all of them on a page, labeling each item. Then photocopy the whole page. (Note that, when photocopying photographs or drawings, it is a good idea to ask for color photocopies. Even black and white photos reproduce more clearly on a color photocopier.) You can also use a computer. Just scan in photos and clippings or copy some from the Internet, arrange them in Adobe Photoshop or a word processing program, and then print them. Many libraries now offer free access to scanners and printers can be bought with built-in scanners and copiers, which can help you put your photos and drawings into digital format.

Another idea is to include illustrations and pictures throughout your autobiography. If you are explaining what a cream separator, a Dictaphone, a party line telephone, a rumble seat, a Rolodex, or a VCR is, you might photocopy a picture of the item and insert it. If you write about buttonhooks, zoot suits, bobby socks, poodle skirts, bell-bottoms, parachute pants, and "grunge" style—or even Mamie Eisenhower bangs, a Jackie Kennedy pillbox hat, or a Farrah Fawcett haircut—pictures may help children of later generations understand exactly what you are talking about.

If you draw or paint, you might include sketches and illustrations throughout your autobiography as well.

READING SUGGESTIONS

•❖ *The Country Diary of an Edwardian Lady* by Edith Holden— This personal journal, begun in 1906, was only recently discovered and published. Much of its charm is the result of Holden's artistic ability. Her paintings of birds, flowers, butterflies, and trees reflect her deep love of nature.

THE MIDDLE YEARS

"No matter how old a mother is she watches her middle-aged children for signs of improvement." —Florida Scott-Maxwell

Life begins at 40: This may seem like a cruel joke, but as we get older we realize that, although not exactly true, life certainly goes on. What was life like for you between your 40th and 65th birthdays? Tell about these years, and remember to be specific and include lots of detail. Even if you don't think of these years as particularly memorable, you'd be surprised at how much you've done—and how much your children and grandchildren would like to read about it.

- What did you look like as a mature adult in your middle years? How did you change, physically, from your younger years?

- Did life "begin" at 40? Was it "nifty" being 50? What about 60? What personal activities were important to you during the 25 years between ages 40 and 65?

- Tell about five significant events in your middle years.

- Tell about the middle years of your marriage. Did your relationship change in any way? How did your romance fare? Are you still together, even now? If not, did anyone new come into your life?

- Did you or someone you know experience a midlife crisis? Do you have any advice for handling such a crisis?

- People often lose their parents in their middle years. How did the death of one or both of your parents affect you? Share your thoughts and feelings about this loss.

- What was it like to watch your children grow into teenagers, or adults? What was it like to have your children move away from home for the first time? How did you feel?

- Put yourself in history. What was it like to live during the various presidential administrations of your life? What major historical events took place during this time?

- What lessons did you learn between youth and middle age? How did you learn them, and what effect did they have?

- Did any of your attitudes, goals, values, or convictions change in the years from ages 40–65? How did they differ from those of your young adult years?

READING SUGGESTIONS

●◆ *Ladder of Years* by Anne Tyler—Tyler tells the story of a 40-year-old woman who goes through a midlife crisis and, in the process, learns more about herself and more about life.

IN THE WORDS OF REAL PEOPLE

My first thought about the middle years of my life is that nature does not always know best. Middle age and teen-agers are like children with matches—combustible. My daughters stepped on my values, questioned my authority, tried my patience. Their teenage years seemed far more turbulent than mine had been, but the absolutes of my age were being torn down on almost a daily basis. Premarital sex, drugs, and career options were just some of the choices they had to make, and there was little I could do to help.

After the girls left home, a new phase of life began for my husband and me. Conversation no longer centered around the children; hobbies came out of the closet; travel brochures cluttered the coffee table. After 20 years of giving, we could be selfish again—one of the few recompenses for middle age.

Virgil wrote, "Death twitches at my ear. Live, says he, for I am coming to get you." And that is what middle age is—a period in which to live before the infirmities of old age creep up on you.

I think of life as a marathon. At some point along the way, we hit the "wall"—a midlife crisis, if you will. Once we pass through this wall, we can progress with dignity into old age.

Have I had a midlife crisis? You bet. It was precipitated by a harmless comment when I was serving on a neighborhood committee. During the meeting I asked a question of one of the members. "Yes, ma'am," she replied. "Ma'am?" I recoiled in shock. I had lived in the South long enough to know when that expression is used. It is either in deference to an authority—which I was not—or in deference to an older person, which I was. Until then I hadn't considered age a factor in my relationships, but obviously for some people it was. Poor me. I mopped the floor with my chin for days, but that didn't help. I didn't get any younger, and it wasn't any fun. So I decided to accept life as it is.

Iva Bjorneby

I suppose that 45 is the peak year for middle age. I remember being at a party at the chaplain's home soon after my 45th birthday in 1967. A friend said that she, too, had just turned 45, and had then realized that she was halfway to 90. Until then I had coped with my birthday pretty well . . . but Ellen's comment really jarred me.

Sue Schulze, *No Fun Like Work*

Maybe it was the year when all my clothes seemed to have shrunk a size or two (and there were many of them), or maybe it was the year when I realized that I didn't wear my shirts tucked into my slacks, seeming to prefer them on the outside to hide the bulge more evident than usual. Maybe I puffed a little more as I went up the stairs, or maybe the steering wheel consistently caught on my buttons. Whatever was ailing me, my boys decided to help me remedy the situation by consolidating their little bit of dollars and presenting me with the ultimate in Christmas presents—a stationary bike. Though chagrined that they obviously had been aware of my tortured seams, I was delighted that they thought me agile enough to mount this contraption and pedal my way to a sylph-like figure. I thought fleetingly that reducing my intake of food would have been a cheaper alternative but immediately rejected that thought. The workout would be so much more dramatic.

At the other end of the scale (an ugly word), I felt more than a little insulted to receive from my realistic sister-in-law, that same Christmas, a little white shawl—one of those affected by the elderly to wear under their coats on an especially cold day. It was a vest-like bit of thing, which had no back but buttoned snugly over the chest and upper abdomen. I didn't know whether to laugh or cry as I surveyed the contrasting gifts. The boys thought there was life in the old girl; my sister-in-law had me over-the-hill. I decided that the situation had its funny side and that I would wear the shawl while pedaling the bike. And I did!

Marietta Hetherington Neumeister

Those were the months when I wasn't sure I was seeing a light at the end of the tunnel or if it was a train coming out. My friend Janet who lived across the ditch from us came over one afternoon when I was especially down in the dumps, and we talked for awhile while I was weeding the garden. She left and returned a couple of hours later with a paper bag. On it was written *A get Bernie's head out of a bag bag*. Inside the paper bag was a bottle of stress vitamins, two magazines with articles about self care, two paperback books—*How to Stop Worrying and Start Living*, by Dale Carnegie, and another about someone who became a success against all odds—and a quart of double chocolate ice cream! I got the message. I began to become more positive after reading and outlining the Carnegie book. What a special gift!

Bernie Bliss, Roots, Blossoms, Wings

FIVE FOR FIVE

"To practice five things under all circumstances constitutes perfect virtue; these five are gravity, generosity of soul, sincerity, earnestness, and kindness." —Confucius

We seem to enjoy the number 5, so here are five questions dealing with fives! These questions present an opportunity to sum up your life thus far, and will help you get ready to write about the rest.

- What were the five most exciting, wonderful things to happen to you as a child? What were the five most dreadful? How about as a young adult or in middle age?

- What are five things you've done that no one would look at you and imagine you've done?

- After you die, if you could come back to earth for 5 days, where would you go? What would you do? Who would you see, and what would you say?

- Who are the five people in your life that influenced you the most? How did they help shape you into the person you became?

- Think of one important event that happened for every 5 years of your life: at age 5, 10, 15, and so on. Which years are the easiest to remember? Which are the hardest? Why?

READING SUGGESTIONS

- *The Five People You Meet in Heaven* by Mitch Albom—This book provides an interesting look at the unknown impact a man had on five people during his life.

LIFE'S HIGHS AND LOWS

"Those who don't know how to weep with their whole heart, don't know how to laugh either." —Golda Meir

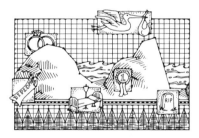

What have been the high points in your life? The low points? Looking back over your past, draw a graph of your life's highs and lows.

Use the center of the page for "average" times. Then plot high points above that line, and low points below it. Connect the points to complete the graph. Be sure to label each high and low point and include its approximate date.

Highs are often events like graduation, marriage, births, and awards. Lows can be periods of sickness, major disappointments, moves, and deaths of family members and friends. Here is an example of one man's graph. (And remember, as a matter of diplomacy, it is a good idea to place the births of your children and grandchildren at equal heights!).

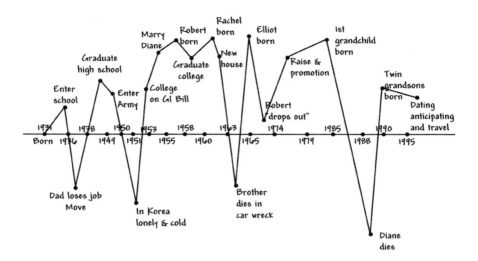

Another idea is to make a more complex chart, using different colored lines. One line might represent emotional highs and lows of your life, while another might represent physical highs and lows, or spiritual highs and lows. (A high point in a woman's life both emotionally and spiritually might be the birth of a child. However, that might be a very low point for her physically.)

Making a chart like this is a complicated process and it necessitates a great deal of thought. However, it can be very revealing.

MAP OF LIFE

"Life is either an adventure, or it is nothing." —Helen Keller

What places in the country—and perhaps the world—have significance for you? Where have you lived? Where have you traveled? Where do your children and other close relatives live?

Photocopy or print out a map of the United States and/or maps of other places in the world that hold significance for you.

Then color in or label the map to mark important places in your life. You might want to include the following places on your map:

- Place of birth, with date

- Places you have lived, with dates

- Places you have visited (color in the states or countries you have visited, and include the approximate dates you were there)

- Places where your children live

- Places where your relatives and close friends live

- Places from which your ancestors emigrated

- Other significant places

Some people color code their maps, using one color for places they have visited, another for places they have lived, another for places their relatives live, and so on. Decide on a plan that works best for you, and remember to include a key. An example of how a finished map might look is provided on the following page.

Key:

● Place of birth:
• Wichita, Kansas; April 3, 1935

≈ Places lived:
• Wichita, Kansas; 1935–1950
• Enid, Oklahoma; 1950–1963
• Sacramento, California; 1963–1968
• Denver, Colorado; 1968–present

★ Places visited:
• Washington; 1948
• England; 1970
• New York, Massachusetts, Pennsylvania; 1979
• Hawaii; 1992

◆ Places children live:
• Patty: Pocatello, Idaho
• John: Bozeman, Montana
• Lydia: Pueblo, Colorado

■ Place mother lives:
• Rocky Ford, Colorado

◉ Places from which ancestors emigrated:
• maternal grandparents: Berlin, Germany
• paternal great-grandparents: Ireland

JUST FOR FUN

*"What a wonderful life I've had! I only wish
I'd realized it sooner." —Colette*

Look over the following just-for-fun questions. Some of them may inspire you to think about yourself in unexpected ways, and will help you reveal aspects of your personality that may not otherwise shine through!

- If you could be anyone—other than yourself—during any time in history, who would you choose to be? Why?

- What is your favorite time of year or season? Why? Did Mother Nature ever interfere or intervene in your life in a significant way? Explain.

- Have you ever seen a forest fire or a house on fire? Have you ever experienced a flood, tornado, dust storm, or hurricane?

- What is your favorite time of day? Are you a morning person? Or are you a night person? Has this changed over the years?

- In what sort of situation or environment are you most comfortable? Least comfortable? What do you do when you find yourself in an uncomfortable situation?

- What are the weirdest experiences you've ever had? What have been the most absurd events of your life?

- Do you have any tattoos? If you were to get one tomorrow, what would it be of? Where would you put it?

- What is your favorite spot in the entire world? Describe it. Why do you like it so much?

- What are your "wow" songs? A "wow" song is a song with a certain combination of lyrics, melody, and attached memories that triggers a strong emotional reaction every time you hear it.

•◆ Do you dream? Do you remember your dreams, understand them, or learn from them?

•◆ We all know things—deep down know them—and often for no good reason. Some people know that there is life on other planets, that they have lived previous lives, or that wearing a certain pair of socks will bring a basketball victory. What do you just know, deep down inside?

•◆ What was the fanciest party you've ever been to?

•◆ What was the most fun you've had in a single day? Describe that day in all its glorious detail.

•◆ What was the most beautiful sunrise, sunset, waterfall, or other scenic view you've ever witnessed?

READING SUGGESTIONS

•◆ *The Earth Is Enough: Growing Up in a World of Flyfishing, Trout, & Old Men* by Harry Middleton—Middleton's protagonist arrives in San Francisco, scarred from the Vietnam War. On a bus trip to visit his grandfather in West Virginia, he meets a time traveler, a woman who claims to have lived a number of lives.

LEISURE TIME

"People are always good company when they are doing what they really enjoy." —Samuel Butler

How have you spent your leisure time over the years? What you do in your down time says a lot about who you are. Some people get antsy and keep themselves busy at all hours of the day, either working or doing work for fun. Others just want to relax and watch TV. Talk about what you do when you're off the clock and you can do anything you'd like to do.

- Is it hard or easy for you to relax? Is it important to you to "play?" How do you spend your leisure time, both now and in the past?

- Has participating in games been important to you—softball, bowling, bridge, tennis, etc.? Explain.

- What religious, social, political, cultural, or other organizations have you been active in? Describe your involvement in them and their meaning to you.

- Have you traveled? Where have you gone? What have you seen? What have you gained from the experience?

- What hobby or hobbies have you enjoyed? How did you get involved? Where has the hobby led you?

- If you have a talent or special gift, how have you used it during your lifetime? What pleasure has it brought you? What pain?

READING SUGGESTIONS

- *Boy* by Roald Dahl—This is Dahl's autobiography, and it's worth reading if just for his description and definition of what an autobiography is!

IN THE WORDS OF REAL PEOPLE

What is my "favorite spot in all the world?" I'm not really surprised that I readily chose my house and acreage north of Ault, CO.

I've been in many places in other states. I've been in Japan and part of the Soviet Union. I visited the Costa del Sol of Spain and viewed the Rock of Gibraltar. I've toured North Africa, sailed the Mediterranean and Caribbean Seas, and ridden in a gondola in Venice. I've viewed Cuba from Key West after crossing from Florida on that wonderful highway over the water, and I've walked on glaciers in Alaska. I've viewed the Temple of the Sun in Mexico. I've admired the handsome people in Portugal. So why do I choose my home?

It's not elegant—there are many grander in the area. It has been remodeled and added to and diminished by the deaths of some of its occupants. It causes me anguish and pain because I can't have all the flowers that used to bloom in its flower beds. I worry about the domestic water pumps and about the expense of upkeep of all the buildings, lawns, and sprinkler system. Yet I don't put it on the market and move to Greeley or to Virginia to Cynthia and Jim's.

Why? Because it's full of good and happy memories. It's comfortable, and I believe attractive. It's peaceful and welcoming. My cat, Pete, and I are happy here. After a long day of meetings in Greeley, I'm glad to come home. After I've been away on a trip I'm glad to come home. Even though I'm often lonely, I'm glad to be here.

Hazel Chick, *Memory Is the Haunting of the Heart*

I have not much to say about love. Today it is a much bigger factor in my life than it used to be. When one gets to be a senior, I believe he or she understands that love comes in more colors and shapes than it used to. It is not a passionate embrace in the back seat of the old sedan. It is enduring life together, taking care of one another, and getting through the boring and repetitive little rituals of life each day that we suffer. It is having a grandchild to lavish kisses upon, to lavish the attention that you failed to give your own son or daughter or spouse. I selected one good and one bad spouse, and I feel very lucky that the good one is still with me. Love is learning not to whimper, whine, and pout. Love is the full expression of your personality while at the same time taming your tongue and understanding others.

Carroll Arnold, *Nothin's Easy*

It all started with a rather nice accordion I saw at a flea market. I bought it for $90, thinking it would be a neat thing to learn to play. At that time I was 76 years old! What's more, I never had a lick of musical training of any kind—sheet music looked like bird tracks to me. I cast about and found someone willing to take me on as a student.

I dreamt, or hoped, that I would be a "natural," one of those guys who picks this stuff up with ridiculous ease and is soon a virtual virtuoso. Hah! Not so. A year and a half later, I have plowed through four instruction books of the Dick Bennett course and find it really tough going. I have developed a healthy respect for any musician who can coax music out of any instrument, something I used to take for granted. I am really determined to whip this thing, and I suppose you would ask how do I feel about it now?

Well, the truth is, I have enjoyed just about every minute of it. It's getting so I can squeeze out some fairly nice music. I can do a creditable rendition of "Dark Eyes" committed to memory. My hope is to enlarge my repertoire way beyond that, and practice one to two hours a day. I guess that is what it takes to get there.

Maybe it is true that it is never too late?

Paul W. Clancy, *Well, I Thought It Was Interesting*

Do you suppose it was just a joke? My daughter, Bonnie, gave me a roll of duct tape for Christmas a couple of years ago. I took the hint and tried hard to keep advice behind a taped mouth . . . unless someone asked for my opinion. Now, guess what . . . I am needing a new roll of tape. Do you think I might get one for Mother's Day?

Bernie Malnati, *Is That the Truth, Mom,*
or Did You Make It Up?

FOOD

A lot of living revolves around preparing food, sharing food, and thinking about food. To eat is to fulfill a basic necessity, and is one of the most universal of pleasures. Food is featured in thousands of cookbooks and scores of diet books; it is indeed well covered by the written word. It is time to add to the stew with your own thoughts and words. The following questions may be inserted into other sections of your writing, or you may wish to include an entire chapter on food alone.

- What is your favorite restaurant meal? What is your earliest memory of a restaurant meal?

- What, if any, recipes are you "famous" for? What do you remember as your mother's specialty? Your grandmother's?

- What is your comfort food?

- What tastes do you crave from your youth? Were there foods you were forced to eat that you hated as a youth?

- Did you ever have a memorable meal on a train? Tell about it. Where were you going? Have you ever had food on an airplane?

- What is the perfect lunch? Your favorite snack? What fruits and vegetables do you prefer?

- How do you like your eggs cooked?

- What is your favorite Campbell's soup? Favorite salad dressing? Favorite flavor of ice cream? Favorite pie?

- Have you ever eaten at a soda fountain, in a teenage hangout with a jukebox?

- Do you think fast food was a positive development? What was the first fast food drive-in you went to, and where was it?

- Write about the five most memorable meals you've ever eaten. Why were they so memorable? Were they particularly delicious, or were they memorable because of the people you shared the meal with?

> ●● What was the most successful meal you ever prepared? Why?

> ●● What is the worst meal you've ever eaten? Describe it.

READING SUGGESTIONS

●● *The Jungle* by Upton Sinclair and *Fast Food Nation: The Dark Side of the All-American Meal* by Eric Schlosser—These two muckraking exposés can help you think about the role food plays in broader social contexts.

●● *. . . And Now Miguel* by Joseph Krumgold—This novel about sheepherders in New Mexico includes a story about that wonderful moment of a meal when a child is invited to sit and eat with the grown-ups.

CHANGES, CHANGES

"There is nothing permanent except change." —Heraclitus

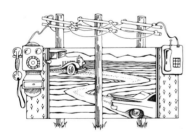

Any adult alive today has seen many changes in the world. You have become experts of change: how to accept changes, cope with changes, survive changes, and flourish under changes. Many readers have lived through the Civil Rights Movement; the women's rights movement; the sexual revolution; the ascension of the U.S. to the world's foremost superpower; the *Baker v. Carr* case establishing "one person, one vote"; the end of colonialism; the environmental movement; and the advent of computers, to name some. These are huge cultural and political changes. You are experienced and need to share your wisdom of how to live through changes, because your descendants will most certainly experience changes in their lives, too.

- What inventions have had the greatest impact upon your life? What inventions are you most grateful for? Least grateful for?

- Other than technological advances, what are the most exciting and positive changes you have seen take place in the world? What are the most alarming and negative changes? Think about changes in society, attitudes, customs, values, and gender roles as you answer these questions.

- What changes do you anticipate the future will bring? How do you think young people can prepare themselves for the changes they will experience—if at all?

- The role of America in the world has changed drastically in the past 100 years. What are your thoughts about this changed role?

Not only have you witnessed amazingly huge changes in your life, but your body has also changed significantly. Think about your body and all that has happened to it over the past 50 or 70 or 90 years. On the sketch of the body shown on p. 125, mark all the changes that have occurred. Be sure to include the dates when and even the geographical sites where these things happened to you. Caption this body with your height and, if it doesn't bother you, with your weight as well.

To help you think about your body's changes, you can answer the following questions by drawing on the diagram, or by making a drawing of your own.

- Have you ever had stitches? Mark them with pound signs.

- Have you ever broken a bone? Mark that with plus signs.

- Do you wear glasses or a hearing aid? If so, draw them.

- Have you had an operation? Mark the areas with triangles.

- Have you had dental surgery? Draw lines to the locations and label the procedures.

- Have you given birth? Write the names of your children on the stomach.

- Have you had anything removed? Your gallbladder? Appendix? Mark it with an X.

- Do you suffer from rashes? Allergies? Chronic condition? Depression? Color the areas red.

- Has your heart ever been broken? If so, feel free to draw your heart in, and add some cracks to it (and hopefully some stitches, if you've shown signs of recovery!).

This schematic diagram will become an entire story. If you have not written about any of the information you've just filled in, you should do so. Our injuries, though painful, often make for wonderful stories!

READING SUGGESTIONS

- *Roots: The Saga of an American Family* by Alex Haley—In this Pulitzer Prize-winning book, Haley records stories of his family, passed down orally through seven generations. The saga begins with an African ancestor who is enslaved and brought to America in 1767. In telling about this man and his descendants, Haley also describes a changing world.

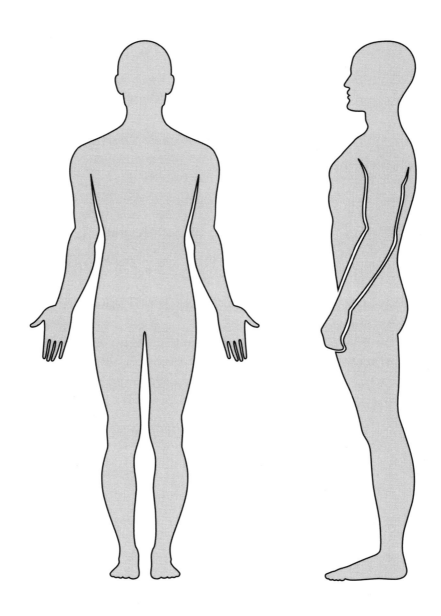

THOUGHTS ON FRIENDSHIP

"Friend: One who knows all about you and loves you just the same." —Elbert Hubbard

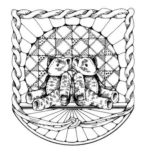

According to Robert Louis Stevenson, "A friend is a present you give yourself." No matter what your age, friends are very precious and important. Reflect upon all the friendships of your lifetime. You may even want to use this opportunity as a good excuse to give them a call!

- Of all your associates and acquaintances, who have been your closest friends? Tell a bit about each of these special people: When were you friends? What did you do together? What kinds of support and/or companionship have you given each other?

- What do you value most in a friendship? What kind of people do you choose for friends?

- What do you think you give to your friends? What do they see in you?

- Have you ever been deeply hurt by a friend? How did you handle that?

- Within your family, who has been your best friend? Explain.

- If you have attended high school, college, or military reunions, describe your feelings about the events. What was it like to see old friends and acquaintances you hadn't seen in years?

- Thinking back, if you had it to do over again, is there anyone you'd like to have punched in the nose, but didn't? Who? Why?

- What is the nicest act of human kindness you've performed? What is the nicest act you've benefitted from?

•◆ *Fried Green Tomatoes at the Whistle Stop Cafe* by Fannie Flagg— In this novel, a woman in a nursing home tells a middle-aged woman an engrossing story about two lifelong best friends. In the process, she helps transform the middle-aged woman's life.

RETIREMENT YEARS

"If I'd known I was gonna live this long, I'd have taken better care of myself." —Eubie Blake

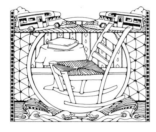

Life from age 65 onward presents both gains and losses. These ups and downs have a different flavor than those of youth, however. Old age brings moments of particular sadness, but especially poignant sweetness as well. Use the following questions as a guide to help you write about your later years:

•◆ What benefits have you found to getting older?

•◆ What losses have you experienced—loss of job, loved ones, good health, independence, etc.? How have you learned to adjust?

•◆ How did you feel about your retirement and/or the retirement of your spouse? How did you adjust to a different lifestyle?

•◆ Did you set goals when you retired? If so, what were they?

•◆ How do you feel about becoming what society calls a "senior citizen"?

•◆ Tell how each of your children "turned out" when he or she left home. What difficulties did each encounter? What successes? Where is each child living now? What is each doing?

◄► Are you a mother- or father-in-law? If so, how does that make you feel? Tell about your sons- and daughters-in-law. When did they enter your family? What have they added to your family? What problems have resulted?

◄► Are you a grandparent? If so, tell about each of your grandchildren. Describe the joys of being a grandparent, as well as the difficulties.

◄► What new activities are you involved in? What new thoughts do you find yourself having? What will you do next?

READING SUGGESTIONS

◄► *Balsamroot: A Memoir* by Mary Clearman Blew—Blew writes about her aunt, a fiercely independent woman who struggles with age. The book is filled with wonderful passages about boxes of unsorted photographs, about longing for love, and about being a child and being a parent.

IN THE WORDS OF REAL PEOPLE

This is my birth month, and I am experiencing very mixed emotions. I'm glad to have been permitted to live these past 75 years, but I'm dismayed to know that in those years I have lost much of myself.

My mind plays tricks on me, which I refrain from speaking about. My eyes have dimmed, so I now miss much about me. I hesitate to ask what it is that my ears don't quite hear. My balance is more uncertain. I no longer climb up on chairs or ladders to reach things. I now look for the guardrails, and I am more fearful of traffic on the street. My teeth don't fit quite right. I find myself foregoing foods I used to enjoy. The ability to control the body functions is lessened. Embarrassed, I begin to retreat into myself.

Things once so important have lost their importance. Today I might be feeling sad at the loss of those things. Tomorrow I might be defiant, telling myself it doesn't matter that I never became a famous ballet dancer or an opera singer, that I never married a doctor, played a violin, or learned to swim or ride a bicycle.

I used to wonder why folks, as they grow older, get so testy about bathing. Now I know! The unclothed body, once so firm and fit, is now seen as flabby and unseemly. I see in the younger people what I used to have, and in the older people what I have yet to lose. It is harder to get in and out of the bathtub, and it is embarrassing to ask for or accept help.

As I was sitting at the kitchen table this morning, lost in musings, I became aware that I was sitting and holding my coffee cup in the exact same way my mother used to hold hers. Tears came to my eyes, and I seemed to hear her say, "It's all right, Mary, all is well."

Mary Koenig, *My Story*

One of the benefits of living a long time is having my adult children become friends. Oh, I know they still carry what we might call parent-child-sibling garbage from the past. But they recognize it for what it is. Our family get-togethers abound in good conversation with lots of laughter. Despite my failings, they love me and show it in their concern for my welfare and pleasure in my company.

Soon, I will have lived for eight decades. I've learned that out of loss comes renewal, and that, for oneself and others, brings happiness.

Lois Osborn, *Eight Decades*

I have had lots of joy in my life, and I hope to have more. Hate is out of the picture in my twilight years. Hate never got me anywhere.

Peggy Hess, *Bits and Pieces of My Life*

As I filled my little plastic pill case for the upcoming week this Saturday, it occurred to me that I was performing an act of faith in the future.

In the spring of 1987, when my allotted physical time on earth expired, by the grace of God and expertise of physicians, I was granted an extension. Of course, I still thank Him at the end of each day for the "day just passed." And thank Him each morning for "another night."

That is being thankful for what has just transpired. The act of faith in the future happens each time I refill my little plastic pill container. In 1987, when my list of medications got to be so long that I had to write them in my little book, I began to forget to take them sometimes.

My cardiologist and I had a discussion about this, and we decided the best thing, in my case, was to arrange for me to take MOST of the pills at the same time each day. I got a plastic case marked S-M-T-W-T-F-S, one letter over each small bin, but each one big enough to hold the medications for the day. After I take the Saturday dosage, I refill the case. I count seven doses of each medication, one at a time, into my hand. Then, I say, to myself. "Sunday, Monday, Tuesday, Wednesday, Thursday, Friday, Saturday," as I drop a dose into each bin.

The process is repeated for each medication, until I have loaded the case for the coming week. Then, as I count the number of pills in each bin and snap it shut, I think to myself, "I'm all set for another week!" Faith in the future.

I put a lot of faith in a little bit of plastic, because I'm bound to each succeeding 24 hours by an abiding faith in the strength of plastic. In addition to the heart bypass operation the surgeons "gave" me, they also replaced the aortic valve with a *plastic* one. Thank God for plastic.

I remember in days past, when I would curse the plastic parts that were attached to steel, around different parts of some of the automobiles that I tried to fix. When plastic and steel do separate, replacement is the only solution. Anyway, I no longer curse plastic . . . for plastic makes MY world go around!

Robert Vail, *Dew on a Leaf*

EVERYDAY LIFE NOW

"Fifty years is a long way to look ahead, but looking back it doesn't seem any time at all. Makes you wonder what life's all about." —Rosamunde Pilcher

Congratulations! You're here, writing the story of your life, and you've made it all the way to p. 131! You're almost there! You should feel very proud of yourself. But, to truly present an accurate picture of yourself, you should take a moment to think about the things you enjoy now. Besides working on your autobiography, how do you spend your days? As always, be honest.

- What are the personal landmarks in your daily life? The places you always go? What kind of stores do you like to wander in—hardware stores, bookstores, cooking shops, gift shops?

- What is the first thing you see when you open your eyes in the morning? What is the first thing you usually think about?

- What routine do you take at night before you turn in? Do you lock the door, and get the coffee pot ready? What do you usually think about as you are drifting off to sleep? Do you sleep well?

- Is there someone you talk to every week? Eat with once a month?

- What is your weekly schedule like? Bridge, golf, class, church? Coffee with a friend? Do you still work for a salary or wages? Do you exercise? Perform charity work? Or are you often babysitting your grandkids?

- Do you read the Letters to the Editor in the newspaper? Have you ever written one?

- How do you laugh? Do you laugh with your whole body? Is it a belly laugh? Do you snort or giggle, let loose a loud "ha!", or a small "tee hee"? What makes you laugh?

How do you cry? Silent crocodile tears, sobbing, or sniffling? What makes you cry? How often do you find yourself crying?

If money and health were no problems and you could choose any activity that pleases you, how would you spend your time? Has this changed over the years? How would you have answered this question 35 years ago?

When you look in the mirror, are you sometimes surprised?

READING SUGGESTIONS

Blackout by Connie Willis—This novel presents an extremely interesting notion about historians. The author, an award-winning science fiction writer, suggests that historians are time travelers, as they go back in time. Her historians living in 2060 return to London in 1940 to record and observe the Blitz. Writers of autobiographies are in many ways time travelers, traveling back in time—sometimes 60, 70, 80 years—to record what happened and, through reflection, to discover why things happened the way they did.

RELIGION AND ETHICS

"It takes a lot more faith to live this life without faith than with it." —*Peter De Vries*

What are your feelings about religion and faith? How would you describe your ethics and values? Now is the time to become philosophical, digging deeper to explain your thoughts on the spiritual and ethical sides of life. Whether you are a regular worshipper or not, we all have systems of right and wrong and of justice that guide our actions and shape our beliefs. Use this time to really think hard about your own ethics and values and how they came to be, how they affected your life, and how they made you into the person you are today.

- Is religion a part of your life? If so, share your religious philosophy and beliefs with future generations. What do you believe? If religion has not been important to you, explain why.

- Have you ever questioned your faith, your God, or your church? Explain.

- Did you ever go through a time of intense self-questioning or self-evaluation when you questioned what you were doing and came out with new goals and purposes?

- Have you explored religions other than the one with which you were raised? What were the results?

- Did you raise your own children in the same church you grew up in? Why or why not?

- Do you have a favorite religious story, verse, song, or prayer? Explain its importance.

- Did any clergy member or theologian or religious leader have an important influence on you? Explain.

- What morals and values are most important to you? If you hold any fundamental truths, what are they?

- Do you believe you've always lived up to your own ethical standards? Have you done anything—or not done something—that you regret?

A FEW MEMORABLE DATES

"I've been on a calendar, but never on time." —Marilyn Monroe

We tend to use dates as hooks, hanging events and feelings on those hooks. It's wonderful how we put historical events into perspective with our own personal and family history.

Think of an important date in history, a date that you remember well. Take yourself back in time. Then write about the date's importance to your life and to the life of our nation. Where were you on that date? What were you doing? How did you feel? Sum up the date's significance to you in a paragraph or two.

Here are a few dates that you might try:

October 27, 1929	The stock market crashes.
December 7, 1941	Japanese forces bomb Pearl Harbor.
April 12, 1945	President Franklin Delano Roosevelt dies.
August 6, 1945	The United States drops an atomic bomb on Hiroshima.

November 22, 1963	President John F. Kennedy is assassinated.
April 4, 1968	Martin Luther King, Jr. is assassinated.
July 20, 1969	Astronaut Neil Armstrong walks on the moon.
August 9, 1974	Richard Nixon resigns as President.
January 28, 1986	The space shuttle "Challenger" explodes.
November 9, 1989	The Berlin Wall is opened to free passage.
April 19, 1995	A bomb destroys the Alfred P. Murrah Federal Building in Oklahoma City.
September 11, 2001	Terrorists fly aircraft into the World Trade Center.
August 29, 2005	Hurricane Katrina hits New Orleans.
May 2, 2011	Osama bin Laden killed by U. S. special forces.

READING SUGGESTIONS

●● *The Book of Laughter and Forgetting* by Milan Kundera—In this novel, Kundera tells a story of a man being "airbrushed out of history" because he fell into disfavor during the communist regime. This is a good reminder how important it is to write your own story and put yourself into history.

IN THE WORDS OF REAL PEOPLE

Elmer, Francie, our toddler, and I were spending the pleasant Sunday afternoon of December 7, 1941, with cousins Sophia and Albert and their family.

Music on the radio suddenly stopped. A terrible announcement filled the room. Pearl Harbor had been bombed. There was a great loss of life and ships. Suddenly the war wasn't "over there"—it was "here," all across our land.

We felt an immediate concern for Sophia's nephew, Leon. He was the finest young man I've ever known. His father, a Quaker minister, was adamantly opposed to bearing arms. Leon was determined to serve his country, so his dad agreed to him enlisting as a conscientious objector.

It was weeks—months after Pearl Harbor—before Leon's parents got word that he had survived the terrible Bataan Death March and was a Prisoner of War held in Japan. Accounts of the inhuman treatment of POWs by the Japanese so consumed the mind of his father that he suffered a nervous breakdown and was placed in the asylum in Pueblo, CO.

The war continued in all its horror, but one midnight hour Leon's father was healed. He called an attendant to ask for his clothes. "I'm well now," he said, "and ready to go home."

When morning came he repeated the request saying, "I'm well now. Last night I saw Leon on a big ship, which was torpedoed. Leon drowned and he is safe now with God." Indeed he *was* well.

Not long after this, the War Department announced that an unmarked ship spotted in the war zone had been destroyed by United States Naval forces. Only when our ships began to pick up a few survivors did the terrible truth come out. The vessel loaded with our own men, who were prisoners of war of the Japanese, had been deliberately sailed into the war zone.

The inhumanity of man knows no limit.

Cleo Wadleigh

Around December 4, 1941, I was sent to Ford Island, a small island in Pearl Harbor with Navy communications on it, to repair a Teletype machine. I was sent in a Navy launch by myself, with just a sailor to pilot the launch. I was struck by the tremendous size and number of ships in the harbor, thinking to myself, "There is no way any country would dare challenge us." I made the repair and went back to Hickam Field, looking forward to December 10, my first year anniversary, with just one more year in the Army to go.

Sunday morning, December 7, 1941, we were all awakened by low flying aircraft, all of us thinking that the stupid Navy was practicing on a Sunday morning. A yell went up from someone that we were being bombed. We all ran outside in our underwear. I looked up into a beautiful blue sky and saw planes clearly marked with Japanese insignia dropping bombs on Pearl Harbor.

Our message center at Hickam Field reported to Fort Shafter that a raid had started. I believe this was the first message of the war.

Around December 11, I was sent back to Ford Island to work on the Navy Teletype machines again. In the launch on my way out to the facility, I passed what was left of Pearl Harbor. Every ship that was still floating following the raid had been ordered out to sea, so all that was left were ruins. Some of the wrecks were still smoking from fires that burned for days following the raid. There were ships' guns sticking up through the water with the waves lapping into them. Comparing the scene to what I saw just a week earlier was mind-boggling.

The raid on Pearl Harbor was the beginning of World War II. My first year anniversary was now meaningless. Everyone in the service was now in until the war was over 4 years later.

Bernie Lynch

On May 4, 1945, I was home alone on the farm except for the children I babysat. The people I worked for had gone to visit the neighbors and listen to the forbidden radio messages from England. Every day we would hear the coded messages England sent to the Resistance groups in Denmark. Of course, I didn't know any of the codes, but we all listened to them anyway. They would be some silly things like, "The gray dove is flying tonight," "The bread is in the oven," "The ship has sailed," or any such message.

So on the fourth, as every other early evening, I was listening to the radio. All of a sudden, everything stopped. No sound from the radio. Then a crying, happy voice came through. "The war is over, we are free!" It is impossible to describe what I felt. I was a 17-year-old girl. The children were asleep, and I just couldn't contain the happiness I felt. I ran laughing out of the house to the nearest neighbor, who happened to be an 80-year-old widow. But we, the 17-year-old girl and the old lady, danced all over the house and yard, laughing and crying at the same time. The relief and happiness we felt was so unbelievably great. The people I worked for never made it home that night. They, together with everybody else in town, were celebrating our freedom from tyranny.

Agnes Clausen, *The Track of the Wooden Shoes*

BRAG PAGE

"Modesty is a vastly overrated virtue." —John Kenneth Galbraith

It's time to brag about yourself. Tell about the achievements, accomplishments, and rewards of your lifetime—and don't be modest. Describe any talents you've put to good use, academic success you've had, sports victories, military medals, job promotions—you name it. Use these questions to help you get started:

- What public awards have you received in your lifetime? Be sure to mention trophies, plaques, certificates, cash prizes, or other awards. Include recognition from schools, clubs, careers, churches, military services, charities, communities, or other organizations.

- What are your talents, large or small? Include anything from playing the piano to being an interesting conversationalist, having a way with animals, or excelling at leadership.

- What special skills help make you unique? Here's the place to include your ability to touch your nose with your tongue, recite the alphabet backward, dance the rumba, or do a great Donald Duck imitation. Have some fun with this one.

- Tell about the moments in your life that have most pleased you, or the times when you have been most proud of yourself. What pleases you about what you did or about what happened?

➺ When other people have complimented you throughout your lifetime, what have they most often said? Tell about your most frequent compliments—and remember, now is not the time to be humble!

READING SUGGESTIONS

➺ *Charlotte's Web* by E. B. White—Wilbur the pig is saved from the butcher's knife because a spider named Charlotte points out his value, spinning compliments like "Some pig!" into her webs. No one can underestimate the importance of recognition!

LIKES AND DISLIKES

"The world is so full of a number of things, I'm sure we should all be as happy as kings." —Robert Louis Stevenson

Everybody has likes and dislikes. What are yours? What still inspires you, after all these years? What still has the power to rile you up? Look at the categories below and list your favorites for each. Feel free to add categories, and you can write short explanations of why you like each item if you want. When you're finished, go back and do the same for your dislikes.

➺ books

➺ television shows

➺ movies

➺ plays

➺ music (styles, songs, or artists)

➺ colors

➺ dances

➺ foods

➺ flowers

➺ holidays

➺ sports

- cities
- restaurants
- Presidents
- people's names

Look back at some of the responses you came up with to the prompts on page 61. Have your favorites changed much? Are there any that have remained the same?

READING SUGGESTIONS

Humans are fascinated with rankings and prizes. We list our favorite movies (Oscars), published writings (Pulitzers and Caledecotts), academic and political achievements (Nobels), musicians, (Emmys), athletes (MVPs), hotels and restaurants (Michelin stars), and theater performances (Tonys). Many towns' newspapers poll their readers and announce the best breakfasts, best pies, best hamburgers, best taverns, and best parks. Use such lists to help you think about your own favorites.

GIVING ADVICE

"If you want to get rid of somebody, just tell 'em something for their own good." —Frank McKinney Hubbard

Americans gobble up "how to" books. We love to read books about how to build the perfect birdhouse, to paint a glorious landscape, to raise bright children, and to keep our marriages vibrant. We buy millions of copies of books that instruct us on how to cope with the loss of loved ones, chronic diseases, alcoholism, and disappointment in love. We seek advice from strangers. Who better to give advice than a family member who has survived and thrived through a lifetime of experiences?

We all love to give advice. Here is your opportunity! What advice do you have for future generations about any of the following topics? If you have advice concerning any other issues, make sure to include that as well.

- getting along with others
- money—both cash and credit
- happiness
- religion
- raising kids
- coping with hard times

- love
- giving
- work
- marriage
- growing older
- politics and political parties

Look at the advice you've given. Have you always followed it? If you had your life to live over, what one thing would you do differently?

IN THE WORDS OF REAL PEOPLE

I regret that I didn't give my children the freedom to move more independently into themselves. One time Guy told Bob that he couldn't ski behind his boat until he got his hair cut. I nagged him to cut it. Bob told me later, "Mama, I was only 12." I wish I had allowed them to grow up a little less restricted, into the children *their* personalities dictated them to be. I didn't allow *myself* to be that person either.

Delia Grubb Martin, *Yesterday*

As I look back, there are some things I wish I'd done.

The night before Dad died, he drove up behind me in his laundry truck and told me he had taken care of the paperwork for me to buy his 1929 Model A Ford. He was so happy and so was I, and I had this sudden urge to tell him I thought he was great, and that I loved him, but I didn't. I never had another chance.

Before Helen died, she was backing out the front door and looked so thin and gaunt and ill. I very suddenly had the urge to put my arms around her and hug her and hold her tight—but I didn't, and I never had another chance.

So many times when I would leave Mom by her apartment door and turn to wave before I left, she looked so small and old and lonely. Each time I would think, "Next time I must hug her and tell her I love her." (She should have been hugged each time I saw her. Why am I so inhibited?)

I hated it so when Eddie bought the Saab with bucket seats. I had always enjoyed sitting close to him, with my hand on his leg, or—on long trips—with my head in his lap. Now I couldn't do this anymore. With so many kids at home, it was nice to be close while driving. I should have told him I wanted a car with a bench seat.

Clare Foster, *Roses and Thorns*

COMMANDMENTS

"A proverb is a short sentence based on long experience." —*Miguel de Cervantes*

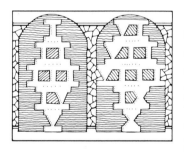

No matter your faith or religion, we all follow commandments—not just of the capital-C variety, but other, less obvious ones, too. These are the sayings, proverbs, and messages that we heard while growing up, usually from our parents. As adults, we are often not aware of how deeply the messages have affected us, or of how much they have become our own.

Here are a few popular maxims that you may recognize:

- ✎ Honest work never hurt anyone.

- ✎ Use it up, wear it out, make it do, or do without.

- ✎ Cleanliness is next to godliness.

- There is only one way to get the milkin' done, and that's to get to milkin'.
- If you can't afford it, don't buy it.
- Let your conscience be your guide.
- Whatever is worth doing is worth doing well.
- If you can't say something nice, don't say anything at all.
- Never leave home without clean underwear.
- Life is what you make of it.
- Go for the gusto/Go for the gold.
- You only go around once/You only live once.
- Make love, not war.

Jot down the proverbs and messages that you heard while growing up. How have these philosophies influenced your life? Who passed them down to you, and what messages would you like to pass down to your own children?

TURNING POINTS

"No trumpets sound when the important decisions of our life are made. Destiny is made known silently." —Agnes de Mille

In all of our lives there are turning points. Sometimes we are not even aware of when they occur. Looking back over your life, think about those moments when you took one path and not the other. Think about how they arose, how carefully you considered your choices, and how your life might have played out differently if you had chosen otherwise.

- What were the turning points in your life? How did these turning points affect you and the people around you?

➥ What change in your life has brought you the most pleasure?

➥ What change in your life has brought you the most pain?

➥ Do you have any regrets about the "what ifs" of your life: What if you had finished college? What if you had taken that other job? What if you hadn't married so young? What if you hadn't been so strict with your eldest child?

➥ Have your views about what is important in life changed? If so, how?

➥ What circumstances helped determine the road you traveled? Consider your family, your community, your country, and the world.

➥ In what period of your life were you most content, happy, and at peace with yourself and your surroundings? Why then?

➥ In what period of your life were you most unhappy, miserable, and confused? Why?

READING SUGGESTIONS

➥ *The World Is My Home: A Memoir* by James A. Michener—In this memoir, Michener describes a turning point in his life when, as a young soldier in World War II, he was faced with death and started to think of the future.

➥ "The Road Not Taken," from *The Road Not Taken and Other Poems* by Robert Frost—Frost explores the concept of choices that "make all the difference."

IN THE WORDS OF REAL PEOPLE

The date was December, 1946. I cannot be more specific, for little did I know that the events of that day would affect my entire life . . .

A group of us went skiing. It was the first time for me. I had poor equipment, but worse than that, no knowledge of skiing. The company general manager, who was a good skier, had observed my skiing and suggested that I put more weight on the tips of my skis. So, on one of my trips down, my last one, I thought of his suggestion and decided to lean forward a little. I'm not sure what I expected, certainly not what happened. Before I knew it, I was falling head over heels, ending up at the bottom of the slope, still in one piece, but obviously injured. An X-ray confirmed that I had fractured my ankle.

I had been working with Maplecrest Turkey Farms, a firm that produced and marketed turkeys. My work varied with the changing scene—winters in the hatchery, spring and summer in the feed mill, and fall in the processing plant. Now, with my leg in a cast and needing crutches to get around, it was impossible for me to work. I reported to the plant to see if there was something I could do. I was told they would find something for me to do in the office and keep me on the payroll.

I must have left some favorable impressions as to my capabilities, for several months later—when I was back at my former jobs—I was asked if I would like to work in the office again and learn bookkeeping procedures. I jumped at the chance, not knowing what to expect. I had never even entertained the idea of becoming a bookkeeper. But I thought, why not?

Well, that was 1947. For the next 40 years, accounting was my profession. I never studied it, but I learned it well in the school of hard knocks. I stayed with the same company for 31 years. There were changes of ownership and mergers, but I just rolled with the punches and ended up being controller for the corporation, a holding company with 11 divisions doing more than 100 million dollars per year.

It all started with a fractured ankle—just a hairline fracture, no big deal, no permanent disability. I don't even remember which ankle. But it affected my whole life.

Eldon Risser, *The Years of My Life*

There was a lightning storm when we lived at 230 North Grant Avenue—in the fall. I was canning peaches at my double kitchen sink. They had been scalded and were ready to peel and put in jars.

The phone rang. It was my brother calling from work to say he'd taken Helen, his wife, to the hospital the night before, and they couldn't tell for sure what was the matter with her. I thought of Helen, remembering how good she'd been to help me during my mother's illness and death.

Something made me wash my hands, take off my apron and go to the hospital.

When I returned home, I found the neighbors in their yards, and one called to me, "Lightning struck close to here!" I looked at our antenna, and it had fallen over. I ran in, and the house was full of smoke. I called the fire department. They came and blew the smoke out with fans. They said the insulation in the attic prevented a fire.

I called the insurance man. He came right away and said, "If you'd been at that sink with your hands in water, you would have been killed!" The pipes around the sink were all burst.

Always after that, whenever I knew I should do something good, never did anything stop me!

Peggy Hess, *Bits and Pieces of My Life*

Over time, I had watched the men and women sit down, put their elbows on a bar, and drown their talents and ambition in beer. I had watched true dramas of human misery. Eventually, tavern training formulated a type of warped illumination far beyond my experience. It was inevitable that my reality would collide with the youthful beliefs of my peers who accepted the illusions of happily-ever-after in Betty Grable movies.

The day after the Fourth of July party at the Cactus Patch bar, I decided to change our nightly routine. "I'm staying home from now on," I announced to my mother as we had just about finished supper dishes.

She pulled her hands out of the soapy water, turned to my dad and said, "What do you think, Jack? Is she old enough?"

He leaned back in the chair and looked up at the ceiling. "Don't see why she can't. We'll be less than a block away if anything happens."

There was no more discussion. I had passed my first initiation into adulthood by saying no. The power of this was extravagant and electrifying. Behind the gift of squandering my youth at the Cactus Patch bar was the strength to step out into the world on my own. Better yet, there was no one to stop me from trying out anything and everything.

Donna Davis, *Dancing in the Cactus Patch*

STAGES OF ADULTHOOD

"The years between fifty and seventy are the hardest. You are always being asked to do things, and yet you are not decrepit enough to turn them down." —T. S. Eliot

In her books *Passages* and *Pathfinders*, Gail Sheehy describes the following stages of adulthood:

- ❧ Pulling Up Roots (ages 18–22)
- ❧ The Trying Twenties (ages 23–27)
- ❧ Catch-30 (ages 28–33)
- ❧ Deadline Decade (ages 46–55)
- ❧ The Freestyle Fifties
- ❧ The Selective Sixties
- ❧ The Thoughtful Seventies
- ❧ The Proud to Be Eighties

What do you think about the way Sheehy describes these stages of life? Can you come up with your own descriptive terms for the decades of your life?

READING SUGGESTIONS

●❖ *Suddenly Sixty and Other Shocks of Later Life*; *I'm Too Young to Be Seventy: And Other Delusions*; and *Unexpectedly Eighty: And Other Adaptations* by Judith Viorst—Viorst, children's author and a wonderful poet, writes a new book of poems as she settles into each new decade of her life. Her poetry is honest, whimsical, and full of humor and wisdom.

IN THE WORDS OF REAL PEOPLE

This is the story of my life, as I remember it. Two people will look at the same rose and have different reactions. One will smell the fragrance and notice the soft folds of the petals. Another might just see the color of the rose and notice the thorns.

So it is with life. We believe what we want to believe. We see what we want to see. We hear what we want to hear.

Living life is not easy. It is taking the lemons we are given and making lemonade that make us flourish and become more perceptive.

Read what you want. Discard what you want. I will still remain one of your ancestors.

Julia L. "Judy" Graham, *My Life*

On January 28, 1988, I will have reached my 77th birthday. I still can't believe I have reached that age.

As people grow older, they have a tendency to relive the past. Some say, "It is over. Never look back." But at my age, I feel that recalling memories is part of living. The nice thing about it is, you don't have to stay at any certain age. You can stray at will throughout all the levels of time. The most pleasant journeys we take in life are back through memory.

So, as the years unfold, take my hand and let's walk through my childhood, my growing-up years, down the steps into a threshold of history.

Marie Giesler, *Sentimental Journey*

When I joined an autobiography-writing class of brilliant brains and world wanderers, it was quickly evident we had little in common. There was, however, one question to puzzle us all—when you begin your life story WHERE do you start? When you were first "hatched" seems logical. But the *Writing Your Life* book gave the best clue—it said "with ancestors."

Since everyone has ancestors of one sort or another, I figured I could do THAT. So—I thought—give it a whirl—can't hurt!

The teacher was a comfort. She was young and dear. When she faced the class for the first time, she turned pink and rather timidly said, "I hope you realize I am accustomed to teaching 8- and 10-year-olds." I understood completely. It was thoroughly intimidating for both of us. But she stayed the course. So did I.

Since the book said, "Start with ancestors," I said to myself, "Let's go!" I may be devoid of degrees and failing as a frequent flier, but I HAVE ancestors!

And I have learned something else from this excursion from the distant past to the noisy present. I have found it is not necessary to go places, to do things, or to be Somebody to have a fulfilling and wonderful life!

Mary Irwin, *Who's Got the Toothbrush?*

I began this chronicle on February 7, 1985 (my 71st birthday), and am now writing this in December, 1985. I have edited and rewritten reams as further memories and observations impinged upon and amplified former, already-written words . . .

Blushing modesty would normally have prevented me from writing at such great length about so many events in my life, were it not for the sake of family history. Some parts are no doubt trivial, and some more vital to proper perspective. I have no editor with a monstrous blue pencil to eliminate the chaff from the wheat. You can be my editor by skimming over the trivial.

Leading busy lives as you do, I can hardly expect you to reply in kind by writing about your childhoods as you remember our part in them, but it would be very interesting to both Mom and me, some day, to have your viewpoint of those crowded days.

Mark Yurman, *My Biography*

I can never explain why I did the things expressed in this autobiography. I really don't know why I did them. Stuff happens.

I've decided to call it *Nothin's Easy*. I just could never do anything the easy way, always the hard. I think being red-headed, the youngest of four brothers, overweight, and a Democrat have all at one time or another retarded my growth and success.

If my spartan style of writing, without too much embellishment, turns you off, I apologize. That's just the way I was trained in journalism school: who, what, when, where and why. This is no literary classic, but it's classically me.

Carroll Arnold, *Nothin's Easy*

HISTORY AND YOU

"History will be kind to me for I intend to write it." —Winston Churchill

You have been writing about the history of your family and yourself for some time now. You have discovered that, no matter what a person's age, writing an autobiography can be an exciting journey back into the past and forward into discovery and self-understanding. Think about commenting on one or all of the following statements.

- ◆ "One faces the future with one's past."—Pearl Buck, author of *The Good Earth* and winner of the 1938 Nobel Prize in Literature.

- ◆ "Life can only be understood backwards, but must be lived forwards."—Søren Kierkegaard, early 19th century Danish theologian, poet, and philosopher.

- ◆ "I think history is to the nation as memory is to the individual and an individual deprived of memory doesn't know where he's been and where he's going."—Arthur Schlesinger,

Jr., Pulitzer Prize-winning historian and a former assistant to President John F. Kennedy.

•◆ "History is a guide to navigation in perilous times. History is who we are and why we are the way we are."—David McCullough, Pulitzer Prize-winning author and historian.

THE FUTURE

"The future belongs to those who believe in the beauty of their dreams." —Eleanor Roosevelt

More and more Americans are living to be 100 years old. The centennial birthday is becoming increasingly common, and people are living productively during their ninth decade of life. Have you considered your future? Choose from the questions below to help you write.

•◆ What do you imagine your life to be like in 5, 15, even 25 years? Where will you live? How will you spend your time? With whom?

•◆ What do you imagine the United States will be like in 5, 15, and 25 years? What problems do you see? How will the world be different from how it is today?

•◆ What problems do you see in your future? What do you think you can do about them now?

•◆ What looks brightest about your future?

•◆ Make a list of what you still need to do. Make a list of what you still want to do—your bucket list!

WHO ARE YOU—REALLY?

"Tell me what you pay attention to and I will tell you who you are." —José Ortega y Gasset

If you are like most people, the face you show the world may disguise your true self, or tell only part of the story. Tell about who you really are: the self inside of you. Describe your hopes and dreams, your philosophies and worries, and everything else that's run through your head for as long as you can remember. Just because you can't see it doesn't mean it's not important. Your ideas are what make you, you.

❧ Describe the intellectual you. What do you like to think about, read about, and learn about?

❧ Describe the spiritual you. What do you care most deeply about?

❧ Describe the emotional you. For example, are you pessimistic or optimistic by nature? How do you feel and show love, hate, joy, sorrow, satisfaction, anger, etc.?

❧ Describe the physical you. What do you look like today? What are your most prominent features? How has your appearance changed?

- What hopes or dreams have you had during your lifetime? Which ones have come true? Which ones have not? What do you still dream about?

- Describe your philosophy of life. You probably have one, even if you have never put it into words. What concepts or principles motivate you? What are the values by which you live?

- What have you had to learn over and over? What are the three most important things you've learned?

- If you could choose a symbol for your life, what would you pick? Why would this symbol describe you?

- What quirks do you have?

- What makes you happy? Has this changed over the years?

- Where do you go when you experience pain, despair, or grief? Inside yourself? Do you join others in groups? How do you grieve?

- Do you think you ended up being the kind of person your parents wanted you to be?

We all have little quirks, such as always putting a sock on the left foot before the right foot, keeping particular dates to put up and take down holiday decorations, making sure the toilet paper hangs a certain way, and so on. Think about your own specific quirks and also how you have learned to live with others' quirks. Make a list of your idiosyncrasies and those of the people around you.

READING SUGGESTIONS

- *Letters and Papers from Prison* by Dietrich Bonhoeffer—A German Lutheran minister writes while in a Nazi prison camp. In his poem "Who Am I?" he wonders, as we all do of ourselves, who he really is.

IN THE WORDS OF REAL PEOPLE

I used to be 5' 5" plus but now have shrunk, as the vertebrae have pulled together, to 5' 4". Yet other people see me as taller than I do, possibly because I try to stand straight to avoid a dowager's hump, and to feel taller. There is a trait in my family called the Serge walk (Mother's maiden name was Serge, and she and all her sisters walked this way, as does my own sister): The body angles forward from the hips, and the shoulders hunch forward as the head lurches along. It should be called the tension trot. I try hard to avoid it. Sneaking a furtive look in a store window glass helps.

My hair is almost totally white now. There is a trace of the original black around the nape of my neck. I still remember the white streak that decorated the front of my hair when I was in high school, years before it became fashionable to paint that streak in with chemicals. (How come eyebrows remain black when the rest of the head hair turns all white?) Maybe that explains my preoccupation with the combination of black and white in the wardrobe I prefer. For years, I made clothing for myself predominantly in black, white, and gray. I even made an afghan in that combination to go with a sofa bed in black-and-white tweed. My car is white with black trim. Am I flaunting my black-and-white flag on top?

Intellectual growth is an ongoing process that seems to accelerate in senior years rather than slow down, in my case anyway. A slow learner? Perhaps I just have more time now to analyze what I am gathering from all the media, books, conversations, and experiences. At least I feel I am freer to absorb what comes my way, retain what is essential or appropriate, and discard what I decide is neither of the latter, or what I frivolously feel is ridiculous or obscenely aggravating. When I was younger and a working mother and wife, there were not enough hours left over for much intellectual anything.

My mother advocated equal rights for women in her high school valedictory speech, then married a physician and devoted her life to his needs. My father was a strict disciplinarian with very high standards of behavior. The conflict those two created in me has resulted in a few major battles and many minor skirmishes between my mind and my heart.

Friends and associates tell me they see in me a strong person with nonconforming originality. I acknowledge the rebellions but not the strength. I see myself as a follower who has been placed in a lead position reluctantly on occasion. I cry at parades, but am depended upon in crises. I give up in the face of authority, but press on in the face of stupidity. I am gregarious, but treasure those quiet times at home.

Who is so brave as to judge which is the real person? The one we think we are or the one the world tells us we are? I feel we present different persons to different groups of people, out of sensitivity or expectations or fears. We could and probably do spend our lifetimes trying to find the answers. That's only part of the fun.

Helene Yurman, *Who Am I?*

If I were to choose a symbol for myself, I think it would be of a not-so-big woman facing life with her head high and a book under her arm, surrounded by all these wonderful people. I would hope that in return, I might offer them love and encouragement.

Hazel Chick, *Memory Is the Haunting of the Heart*

Who am I? I never tried to analyze my life in those terms. I like honesty in people but not to the point that it is hurtful. I'm relaxed around people who are comfortable with themselves enough to let you into their world without that awkwardness of "getting to know you first." I can feel awkward and shy sometimes and outspoken and bold at other times.

I am the image of my mother, certainly in body style. She was a tall woman and carried a little too much weight. I can relate to that. When I look at pictures of her in her later years, it is startling to see how much I look like her. I think our temperaments are the same. I admired her so much that I hope I have been living my life in a manner to which she would be proud.

I am strong on commitment. If I say I'll do something, I'll do it. People not following through on something they promised frustrates and angers me . . .

I find wonderment in reaching out and trying new things. I joined a class turning rocks into gems. I knew nothing about it and was a little hesitant about those polishing and grinding wheels. I tried it and have enjoyed immensely watching a "ho-hum" rock polish into a beautiful stone.

I believe strongly in Maya Angelou's statement, "When people show you who they are, believe them." It's been proven many times over in my life . . .

Joan Milne, And So It Was

Chapter 5
Putting It All Together

"I think I did pretty well, considering I started out with nothing but a bunch of paper." —Steve Martin

BEGINNINGS AND ENDINGS

Before you are finished with your memoirs, you have just a bit more writing to do—the pages for the beginning of the book and the pages for the end. At the beginning of the book, you may choose to add these pages:

- title page
- copyright notice
- dedication
- acknowledgments
- table of contents
- prologue

At the end, you many want to include these sections:

- epilogue

- appendix

- index

Below is more information about what to include on these pages.

TITLE PAGE

On the title page of your book, put the following:

- the title of your book,

- your name, and

- the date the book was completed.

COPYRIGHT NOTICE

Include a copyright notice, if desired, on the back of the title page or on a separate page. The copyright notice should include the following:

- the word "copyright,"

- the copyright symbol: © or (c).,

- the year the work was completed, and

- your name.

Example: Copyright ©2012 by Mary Borg

Copyright is a form of protection for writers. According to current copyright law, your work is automatically protected from the moment of its creation, enduring for your life plus an additional 70 years, whether or not you filed a registration. A copyright registration is simply an official record of the copyright. (Much more information about copyright is available from the United States Copyright Office at http://www.copyright.gov.)

If you would like to register your copyright, you will need to fill out Form TX, available online at the U. S. Copyright Office website. (If you don't have Internet access or are unfamiliar with computers, any librarian should be able to help you find what you need.)

Fill out Form TX carefully. Then include Form TX, two copies of the book or manuscript (with the notice of copyright included on each) and the $45 registration fee, all in the same envelope. (Note: Your books will not be returned). When the material has been registered, you will receive a certificate verifying the registration of your copyright. Don't be impatient. It may take several months to receive the registration certificate.

DEDICATION

The next page is usually the dedication page. To whom would you like to dedicate your book? Perhaps you would like to dedicate it to an individual, to your ancestors, or to your descendants. The dedication page should include a statement of dedication, often something as simple as "For my children."

ACKNOWLEDGMENTS

If you would like, write a statement acknowledging anyone who gave you particular help in preparing your book—perhaps a family member or friend who helped you gather information, locate pictures, or type your manuscript. You might even want to thank the wife, son, or granddaughter who "nagged" you into writing the book in the first place! And if you included words written by someone else—a poem, the words of a song, or a journal, letter, or diary entry from a relative or friend—you must acknowledge the creator of those words by name and, if applicable, the title of the source. In other words, this acknowledgment is a list of thank yous to those who assisted you in writing your life.

TABLE OF CONTENTS

For the table of contents, list the chapter titles and the pages on which they begin. (If you haven't done so already, be sure to number the pages of your book!) This is usually one of the last pages you will create.

PROLOGUE

As you put together the story of your life, consider writing a prologue. The prologue creates a first impression. It sets the tone for the rest of your book. It is generally easy to write, for you have already written the hard part—the book itself.

There are no rules for writing a prologue. Make yours as short or as long as you like, as simple or as complex. Only you know what introductory remarks you would like for the opening of your book. A prologue is an invitation to enter into your book with you, the author. For some sample prologues, see pages 148–150.

EPILOGUE

The epilogue is your opportunity to add a final touch to your story. Like the prologue, it can be as simple or as detailed as you like.

The epilogue might take the form of a blessing to your descendants. It might be a challenge. It might be a prediction. It might even be a promise for a second volume of your work! The epilogue is similar to wrapping a package with a beautiful bow and declaring, "Here is my gift, I hope you loved it!"

APPENDIX

An appendix is for information that doesn't fit anywhere else in your book. It can have several parts, covering a variety of topics.

The appendix might include favorite family recipes or the ingredients for home remedies that your family has found successful over the years. It might include useful bits of family information, like the location of burial plots, the instructions for turning on the water at the mountain cabin, a list of who has what family heirlooms, or the names of the banks in which deeds, wills, and other assets are located.

The appendix might also include copies of documents that provide historical authenticity to your story, like marriage licenses, church confirmation certificates, naturalization or citizenship papers, death certificates, property deeds, or old bills of sale.

The appendix might even include answers to questions that you may find difficult to discuss with family members. Some of those questions might be:

- If you become very ill, what are your medical desires?

- Have you made a living will? If so, where is it?

- Do you wish to be a transplant donor?

- How do you feel about extraordinary life support techniques?

- Are there specific instructions you would like to leave for your burial and funeral or memorial service?

- Where would you like your final resting place to be?

An appendix is not essential for your book, but it can be a very interesting addition to your autobiography.

INDEX

An index is an alphabetical listing of topics and/or names that are mentioned in your book, with the page numbers where they are mentioned. Because compiling an index can be time-consuming, include one only if you feel it is important to your book.

For example:

    travels, 22, 95, 99–102
    Uncle Joe, 10, 12, 72

For those who are skilled with computer programs, many programs include instructions for formatting so that the software will build an index for you automatically.

DETAILS, DETAILS

Before your book is typed, you will need to take care of some details—editing and proofreading. Editing and proofreading are essential to making your book the very best it can be.

EDITING

Editing is the first step in turning your finished material into a book. It involves making any major changes you wish to make, perhaps deleting material, adding material, moving paragraphs around, and/or reorganizing.

The best way to proceed is to sit down and read your work, pretending that you did not write it yourself. Notice and take notes. Ask yourself: Did I include all of the necessary information in each section— dates, places, people's names and their relationship to me? If I were a stranger to this story and was reading it in the year 2050, would I understand everything written? And most importantly, did I describe emotions and write how I *felt*, not just what I *did*? If anything seems unclear, make sure to add information, either into the text itself, or perhaps with footnotes or endnotes (if you are using Microsoft Word or a similar computer program, you should be able to add these quickly and easily).

Editing also involves dividing your story into chapters. Chapter divisions make a book easier to read, and they make it easier for readers to go back and find specific references. Chapter titles also make each part of your book more enticing.

Many writers simply use the sections from *Writing Your Life* as their chapter titles. Others name chapters to reflect the things that are important to them, like travel, religion, or literature. Others base chapter titles upon lifelong interests or hobbies. One woman, for example, gave her chapters the names of quilt patterns. Another used the names of birds. One man used the names of old hymns for his chapter titles, and another simply used spans of years, like 1920–1930 or 1930–1940.

The possibilities are endless. Use your imagination and have some fun planning the organization and/or theme of your book. In doing so, a title for your entire work will probably emerge. For example, you might decide to use "moving" as the theme for your book, because of all the many places you have lived. You could then use different addresses as chapter titles and call the entire book *On the Road Again*.

Choose your title carefully. It is an important first step in grabbing the interest of your readers.

PROOFREADING

Proofreading is the final step before your book is typed. You need to go over your book and make any corrections necessary in spelling, punctuation, capitalization, sentence structure, and so on. After you have gone over it yourself, have someone else go over it again—or even pay a professional proofreader to do it.

It is important to do your best, but don't worry about creating a masterpiece of writing. Your children and grandchildren are sure to love your book, flaws and all.

GETTING YOUR BOOK MADE

At last you are ready to put your material into book form. The process can be broken into five major steps:

- ●◆ Getting your material into print
- ●◆ Reproducing photographs
- ●◆ Choosing a cover
- ●◆ Making copies
- ●◆ Binding the book

GETTING YOUR MATERIAL INTO PRINT

If you have been using a computer for your writing, all you need to do once you are finished proofreading and editing your autobiography is print it out. If you have not been using a computer, you will need to have the material typed. You may want to type it yourself, hire someone to type it, or enlist the help of one of your children or grandchildren.

If you do not know how, consider taking the time to learn to use a computer. Computer word processing programs make typing and editing a breeze. It is easy to learn the basics, and you will be amazed by how much you can do on the computer. Instantly you can correct errors. You can move sentences or paragraphs around. You can delete sentences or paragraphs with just a few strokes of the key. Best of all, you don't have to retype the whole page whenever you decide to change something. All you have to do is make your changes; the page then automatically readjusts itself.

With a computer, you can also easily edit font size, styles, and other elements of design. You can make your chapter titles stand out in large, bold print. You can keep your text simple, or make it look like fancy, pen-written script. Even the most basic computer programs offer a great deal of design options, so you can play around with them and find out the best style and layout for you.

PLANNING AHEAD

If you want to include photographs, drawings, or documents on a page that also includes text, you will need to do some planning. The process is easy if you use a computer and digital files. Simply copy and paste the digital image file into the document and then adjust the text as needed. The text should automatically reflow around the picture, so the computer does most of the work for you. If you are using a computer but don't have digital files, you can insert a box for the photo in your document, print the page, place the photo in the box, and photocopy the page. Then use the photocopied page for your book.

If you are using a typewriter, try this method:

- Place the photograph, drawing, or document where you would like it to be on the finished page.

- Make several photocopies.

➥ Type directly onto one of the photocopies, creating an illustrated page. (The extra photocopies are for insurance, in case
you need to start over.)

When planning your book, it is a good idea to include photographs, drawings, and documents throughout the text—rather than
saving them all until the end. Your finished book will then look more
inviting, and it will be more interesting to read.

REPRODUCING PHOTOGRAPHS

First, you will need to decide how to reproduce the photographs you want to include in your book. Whatever method you use,
remember this: Be sure to include captions for all photographs. Each
caption should identify all of the people in the picture, as well as the
place and approximate date the picture was taken. Also note each
person's relationship to you—maternal great-grandmother, second
cousin, daughter, and so on. What is obvious to you may not be obvious to future generations.

Scanning. If you are using a computer for your autobiography,
the easiest and most inexpensive way to get your photographs into
your document is by scanning. You can scan the photos you would
like to use (or have them scanned for you), and then you can insert
the digital image files directly into your document. If you don't have
a scanner, you can use a digital camera to take photos of your photos,
and then follow the same process.

Photocopying. If you don't have access to a scanner or digital
camera, or you are not using a computer, the next best method is
photocopying. Many photos reproduce reasonably well on a con-
ventional photocopier. It pays to experiment with different settings
on the copier, and with different copiers. Interestingly, you may find
that a color copier often greatly enhances the quality of old black
and white photos.

You can find photocopying centers at stores such as Staples and
FedEx Office. These places allow you to make photocopies for only
a few cents per page. Most even have color photocopiers, which will

reproduce colored materials reasonably well—but at a much higher price. Of course, if you live in a smaller town, you can find photocopiers at many businesses, schools, libraries, and even supermarkets.

Reprints. Another option is to have reprints made of your photographs, so that you can attach actual photographs inside each finished book. (Of course, this can be expensive if you are making many copies of your book.) If you don't have the negatives of some photographs, find a business that will make prints from the photographs themselves.

CHOOSING A COVER

For the cover of your book you have many options. You might choose something simple: perhaps plain, colored cardstock available at a photocopying center or from a printer. You might want to create an original design, photocopying the design onto cardstock. You might want to create a special, personalized cover for each child and grandchild, using your talent for quilting, embroidery, watercolor, or calligraphy. Your choices are limited only by your imagination.

Whatever your choice, try to make the cover something that looks inviting and something that will last.

MAKING COPIES

After your book is typed, decide how many copies of the book you want to have made. Make a list of all of the people who should receive a copy. Remember to count each child, each grandchild, each of your siblings, special people in your life, and perhaps your local library.

Whether you photocopy your book or have it printed, be sure to ask about the availability of acid-free paper, which will preserve your material for a much longer period of time than ordinary paper. You may need to special order the paper or go to an office supply store, but the added quality will be worth the extra effort and expense.

If you have a computer and printer, you may choose to print it all out from the comfort of your home. This is by far the easiest method; though, depending on the number of copies you want to make, the amount of color used, and the speed and quality of your printer, it may take a long time (and a few ink cartridges). If you don't have access to a printer, or would prefer a more professional approach, here are some other ways you can produce your finished work.

Photocopying. Photocopying is a tried and true method of making copies. You can photocopy the pages yourself, or you can have a photocopying center do it for you. If you use a photocopying center, make sure to mention that you want the material collated. Then you won't have to spend time putting the pages in the proper order. Many photocopying machines at such centers will collate the pages automatically.

At a photocopying center, you may be able to combine choosing a cover, making copies, and binding your book into one step. The attendant can show you what kinds of cardstock, paper, and plastic binding are available. You can then have your cover design photocopied onto the cardstock, your book photocopied onto your choice of paper, and the cover copies bound together with plastic binding. Often, copies of your book will be finished in only a few minutes.

Professional printing. If you want a higher-quality reproduction, or if you want to print a large number of copies, consider taking your book to a print shop. The overall cost will be high, but the book will have sharper, longer-lasting print. Your printer will be able to guide you through the steps necessary in completing a printed book.

Be sure to get an estimate for the job before you get your book printed. It is also wise to shop around and compare prices. Many photocopy centers and office supply stores also do custom printing if you send them the digital file for your book or take a CD of your work.

Self-publishing at a print-on-demand publisher. Another route you can take is to have one of the new print-on-demand publishers produce an actual book for you. Virtual Bookworm, Lulu, and iUniverse are just a few examples of companies that provide this service (to find out more about them and others, just look up "self-publishing" on any Internet search engine). If you go this route, you will need to do your homework and investigate your options carefully. Technological opportunities and requirements are changing rapidly in this area. In addition, these options can sometimes become pricey, depending on the style and number of copies you choose.

BINDING THE BOOK

Unless you are using a print shop or print-on-demand publisher, you will need to decide how to bind the pages of your book. The easiest binding, for most purposes, is plastic comb or spiral binding, available at photocopy centers and offset printers for only a few dollars (or less) per book. Simply take in the copies of your books, with the covers, and ask the attendant about plastic comb or spiral binding. The books can often be bound while you wait.

Other options for binding include making handbound books or using three-ring notebooks. With three-ring notebooks, you can encourage family members to add pages to the family history you have created.

If you are using a printer or print-on-demand publisher, you may have the option of having the book either perfect bound or saddle-stitched (stapled in the center), and you may be able to choose between hard and soft cover binding. Talk to your printer about binding possibilities.

If you don't want to spend the time and money necessary to create physical copies of your book, you can also consider simply creating a digital file of your work and sharing that online. If it's not too large, you can e-mail it to your family and friends. Otherwise, you can make use of Dropbox or other cloud-computing services that will host your files, granting anyone with Internet access the ability to read them. You can also make it so that only people you specifically invite have access to your file folders. More information can be found online at http://www.dropbox.com, or just search for "cloud storage" on the search engine of your choice for more options.

KEEP ON WRITING

After you finish your autobiography, congratulate yourself. You should feel proud of your accomplishment.

But don't stop now. You have become a writer. Try writing in a journal on a daily, weekly, or monthly basis. Write about the events of your present day life and about your thoughts and feelings. Or write a second volume of your memoirs, adding more stories from the past or continuing with stories about your life today. Another idea is to experiment with other writing styles, perhaps trying your hand at fiction or poetry.

The more you write, the more you will think of to write about. *Writing* your life can become a *way* of life.

Enjoy it.

Appendix
Decades

"The course of life is unpredictable . . . no one can write his autobiography in advance." —Abraham Joshua Heschel

What was happening in the world in 1927? Or 1952? Or 1974? To help you remember, here are lists of some of the important events of each decade of the 20th century, from 1920–2000, as well as those of the first decade of the 21st century (from 2000–2010). Major events from 2010 through the time of publication are also listed. Key words, names, and phrases accompany the lists, which can be used as memory joggers to help you remember events, fads, and other cultural phenomena of each decade.

THE 1920s

Presidents of this decade:
- Warren Harding (1921–1923)
- Calvin Coolidge (1923–1929)
- Herbert Hoover (1929–1933)

The 18th Amendment, Prohibition, becomes law.

The U.S. Department of Justice's "red hunt" targets radicals and aliens.

The 19th Amendment gives women of the United States the right to vote.

The Teapot Dome scandal is uncovered.

The Ku Klux Klan gains political power in the United States.

Vladimir Lenin dies; Joseph Stalin wins power in U.S.S.R.

John T. Scopes is convicted for teaching evolution in Tennessee public schools.

Nicola Sacco and Bartolomeo Vanzetti are executed.

Charles Lindbergh flies solo across the Atlantic Ocean.

The stock market crashes.

KEYWORDS

A&P

Aimee Semple McPherson

Amos 'n' Andy

Babbitt

Babe Ruth, and his trade to the Yankees

bathtub gin

Bessie Smith

Bill "Bojangles" Robinson

bobbed hair

bootleg liquor

Burma-Shave

buying on credit

"cat's meow"

Cecil B. DeMille

the Charleston

Charlie Chaplin

the Cotton Club

crossword puzzles

crystal set (radios)

Dorothy Parker

Douglas Fairbanks

Duke Ellington

Edna St. Vincent Millay

Ernest Hemingway
F. Scott Fitzgerald
"Fascinating Rhythm"
"Fatty" Arbuckle
the first Miss America contest
flagpole sitting
flappers
flivvers
George Gershwin
"gin mills"
Gloria Swanson
The Great Gatsby
H. L. Mencken
the Harlem Renaissance
the Holland Tunnel
hooch
"I Found a Million Dollar Baby
   (in a Five and Ten Cent Store)"
"I'd Walk a Mile for a Camel"
isinglass curtains
the "It" girl
Izzy (Einstein) and Moe (Smith)
Jack Dempsey
jazz
Jim Crow
Kiwanis
Knute Rockne
Ku Klux Klan
"Ma, He's Making Eyes at Me"
mah-jongg
"Makin' Whoopee"

marathon dances
Mary Pickford
The New Yorker
"Ol' Man River"
Papa Joe Oliver
Pierce-Arrow
Prohibition
"the quest for normalcy"
raccoon coats
"Red" Grange
"Rhapsody in Blue"
Rudolph Valentino dies
rumble seats
"Second Hand Rose"
"Show Me the Way
   to Go Home"
Shuffle Along
"Singin' in the Rain"
Sinclair Lewis
Sonja Henie
speakeasies
St. Valentine's Day massacre
"Stardust"
"talkie" movies
tango
The Ten Commandments
"Toot, Toot, Tootsie!"
vaudeville
Will Rogers
Woolworth's
"Yes! We Have No Bananas"

THE 1930s

Presidents of this decade:
- ➥ Herbert Hoover (1929–1933)
- ➥ Franklin D. Roosevelt (1933–1945)

The Great Depression grips the world.

The Lindbergh baby is kidnapped.

Veterans march on Washington, DC, demanding cash bonuses.

Roosevelt launches the New Deal (WPA, Social Security, AAA, CCC).

Hitler gains dictatorial power.

The Holocaust begins in Europe.

The 18th Amendment, Prohibition, is repealed.

The Dionne quintuplets are born in Canada.

Huey Long is assassinated.

Joe Louis knocks out Max Baer.

Edward VIII abdicates the throne.

The Spanish Civil War breaks out.

The *Hindenburg* crashes.

Amelia Earhart disappears.

The Munich Pact allows Germany to partition Czechoslovakia.

Germany invades Poland.

World War II begins.

KEYWORDS

"A Foggy Day in London Town"
Al Capone
alphabet soup agencies
Amelia Earhart
Artie Shaw
"Baby Face" Nelson
"Beer Barrel Polka"
Benny Goodman
Bette Davis

the "Big Apple"
black sateen bloomers
"Blue Moon"
Bonnie and Clyde
bonus marchers
"Brother, Can You
    Spare a Dime?"
Buck Rogers
Busby Berkeley

CCC boys
the CIO
Clark Gable
Count Basie
Dick Tracy
dust bowl days
E. H. Crump
the Empire State Building
  is constructed
the end of Prohibition
Fibber McGee and Molly
fireside chats
Flash Gordon
Fred Astaire and Ginger Rogers
Gertrude Stein
Glenn Miller
the Golden Gate Bridge
  is completed
Gone With the Wind
The Green Hornet
Greta Garbo
hoboes
Hoovervilles
Huey Long
"I Got Rhythm"
ice men
Jack Benny
"Jeepers Creepers"
Jesse Owens
jive
Joan Crawford
Joe DiMaggio
Joe Louis, the Brown Bomber
John Dillinger
John Steinbeck
Judy Garland
Kate Smith

Knickers
Lindy Hop
Little Orphan Annie
Lux Radio Theatre
"Ma" Barker and her boys
Mae West
marcelled hair
Margaret Mitchell
the Marx Brothers
"Mood Indigo"
"Mother" Bloor
Myrna Loy
Okies
One Man's Family
Orson Welles
Ovaltine
Pearl Buck
peddlers
"Pennies From Heaven"
Porgy and Bess
"Pretty Boy" Floyd
scat singing
Shirley Temple
sit-down strikes
"Smoke Gets in Your Eyes"
Snow White and the
   Seven Dwarfs
soda jerks
squatters
swing
The War of the Worlds
The Wizard of Oz
WPA workers
Young Communist League
"Zing! Went the Strings
  of My Heart"

THE 1940s

> **Presidents of this decade:**
> ➺ Franklin D. Roosevelt (1933–1945)
> ➺ Harry S. Truman (1945–1953)

Japan bombs Pearl Harbor and the United States enters World War II.

The Allies launch the Normandy invasion on June 6, 1944 (D-Day).

The Manhattan Project begins.

Jackie Robinson signs with the Brooklyn Dodgers.

Allied leaders meet at Yalta and Potsdam.

The United States drops atomic bombs on Hiroshima and Nagasaki. World War II ends.

The United Nations is established.

The nation of Israel is established.

The United States conducts the Berlin airlift.

Apartheid is established in South Africa.

The North Atlantic Treaty Organization (NATO) is established.

KEYWORDS

78-rpm records	black markets
A Streetcar Named Desire	blackouts
A Tree Grows in Brooklyn	bobby soxers
"All I Want for Christmas Is My Two Front Teeth"	*Brigadoon*
	car hop girls
argyle	*Casablanca*
Auschwitz	"Chattanooga Choo Choo"
Ava Gardner	Chiquita Banana
Ayn Rand	*Citizen Kane*
B-17 bombers	civvies
the Battle of the Bulge	Coconut Grove
bebop	convertibles
Bill Mauldin's *Willie and Joe* cartoons	Dachau
	Death of a Salesman

Elizabeth Taylor
fake hose seams
Frank Sinatra
the G.I. Bill
G.I. Joes
Gary Cooper
The Glass Menagerie
goodbye weddings
Harvey
hello babies
Hiroshima
the Holocaust
Ingrid Bergman
internment camps
"It's Howdy Doody time!"
Iwo Jima
jitterbug
John Wayne
jukeboxes
K-rations
Katharine Hepburn
the Kinsey Report
Lana Turner
Lend-Lease
LP records
"Mairzy Doats"
Marian Anderson

Marlene Dietrich
Marlon Brando
the Marshall Plan
Okinawa
penicillin
pin-ups
rationing
Rita Hayworth
Rocky Graziano
Rodgers and Hammerstein
Rosie the Riveter
"Sentimental Journey"
Spencer Tracy
Stars and Stripes
Sugar Ray Robinson
"Tokyo Rose"
U-boats
the USO
V-E Day
V-J Day
V-mail
victory gardens
WACs, WAVES, and SPARS
Willie Gillis
"White Christmas"
wraparound skirts
zoot suits

THE 1950s

Presidents of this decade:
- ➥ Harry S. Truman (1945–1953)
- ➥ Dwight D. Eisenhower (1953–1961)

U.S. troops fight in the Korean War.

Senator Joseph McCarthy hunts for Communists.

The Rosenbergs are sentenced to death for selling secrets to Russia.

General MacArthur is removed from command.

Queen Elizabeth is crowned in Great Britain.

Eisenhower announces the first hydrogen-bomb explosion.

Racial segregation in public schools is declared unconstitutional.

Jonas Salk develops a vaccine for polio.

The Warsaw Pact is signed.

Martin Luther King, Jr. leads a bus boycott in Montgomery, AL.

Fidel Castro comes to power in Cuba.

Alaska joins the United States as the 49th state.

Hawaii becomes the 50th state.

KEYWORDS

3-D movies

air-raid drills

American Bandstand

Annette Funicello

Arnold Palmer

Audrey Hepburn

barbecues

Barbie

baton twirling

beatniks

Bermuda shorts

bomb shelters

Carl Reiner

Cat on a Hot Tin Roof

The Catcher in the Rye

the cha-cha

cocktail parties

crinolines

Davy Crockett hats

"Don't Let the Stars
   Get in Your Eyes"

Dragnet

drive-in movies

ducktails

Edward R. Murrow's *See It Now*

Elvis Presley

Frankie Avalon
the Guggenheim Museum
the H-bomb
The Honeymooners
"He's Got the Whole
  World in His Hands"
hula hoops
"I Like Ike"
I Love Lucy
"In the Cool, Cool, Cool
  of the Evening"
J. Robert Oppenheimer
Jack Kerouac
James Dean
Khrushchev
Korea
Kraft Television Theatre
Kukla, Fran and Ollie
Lawrence Ferlinghetti
Leave It to Beaver
Levitttown
"Love Is a Many-
  Splendored Thing"
"Love Letters in the Sand"
Mad magazine
Marilyn Monroe
McCarthyism
The Mickey Mouse Club

Mr. Peepers
Our Miss Brooks
Ozzie and Harriet
pedal pushers
Perry Como
The Phil Silvers Show
pink flamingos
Playboy
poodle cuts
poodle skirts
The Power of Positive Thinking
"Purple People Eater"
rock 'n' roll
the Rosenbergs
sack dresses
saddle shoes
short shorts
Sid Caesar's *Your Show of Shows*
Sputnik
suburbs
"Three Coins in the Fountain"
TV dinners
TV quiz shows
UFOs
uranium
West Side Story
What's My Line?
Willie Mays

THE 1960s

Presidents of this decade:
- ➤ John F. Kennedy (1961–1963)
- ➤ Lyndon B. Johnson (1963–1969)
- ➤ Richard M. Nixon (1969–1974)

The Peace Corps is established.

The United States attempts to invade Cuba at the Bay of Pigs.

The Berlin Wall is constructed.

The United States and the U.S.S.R. come to a standoff during the Cuban Missile Crisis.

James Meredith registers at the University of Mississippi.

The United States enters and escalates the war in Vietnam.

A civil rights rally is held in Washington, DC.

John F. Kennedy is assassinated.

The Beatles "invade" the United States.

Malcolm X is assassinated.

Medicare program begins.

Muhammad Ali is arrested for refusing to enter the U.S. Army.

Israeli and Arab forces fight in the Six-Day War.

Race riots occur in large American cities.

The first human heart is transplanted by Dr. Christiaan Barnard in South Africa.

Martin Luther King, Jr. is assassinated.

Senator Robert Kennedy is assassinated.

Astronaut Neil Armstrong walks on the moon.

An outdoor concert in Woodstock, NY, draws more than 400,000 people.

KEYWORDS

"A Boy Named Sue"	Aretha Franklin
"All You Need Is Love"	"Ballad of the Green Berets"
Adolf Eichmann	Barbra Streisand
Apollo space program	the Beach Boys

the Beatles
Betty Friedan
Black Panthers
"Broadway Joe" Namath
Camelot
Catch-22
Chubby Checker
civil rights
communes
Debbie Reynolds
DNA
"Doves" and "Hawks"
Dr. Zhivago
draft dodging
Eldridge Cleaver
Fiddler on the Roof
Fidel Castro
flower children
The Great Society
Haight-Ashbury
Hair
"Harper Valley PTA"
"Hell no, we won't go!"
Ho Chi Minh
"I Want to Hold Your Hand"
In Cold Blood
Jack Ruby
James Bond movies
Jimi Hendrix
John Glenn
Kirk Douglas
Laugh-In
Lee Harvey Oswald
Maharishi
Malcolm X
the March on Washington
   for Jobs and Freedom

Martin Luther King, Jr.
Medicare and Medicaid
Mickey Mantle
miniskirts
the Monkees
"Moon River"
Motown Records
Neil Armstrong
The Odd Couple
"Ode to Billie Joe"
Omar Sharif
One Flew Over the Cuckoo's Nest
Paul Newman
Portnoy's Complaint
psychedelia
Robert McNamara
the Rolling Stones
Sandy Koufax
the Selma to Montgomery
   march
Sidney Poitier
Silent Spring
sit-ins
Steve McQueen
Stevie Wonder
the Suez Canal blockade
"Teen Angel"
the Tet Offensive
thalidomide babies
To Kill a Mockingbird
Twiggy
Vietnam
Warren Beatty
the Warren Commission
the Watts Riots
"We Shall Overcome"
Woodstock

THE 1970s

Presidents of this decade:
- ➡◆ Richard M. Nixon (1969–1974)
- ➡◆ Gerald Ford (1974–1977)
- ➡◆ Jimmy Carter (1977–1981)

Four Kent State University students are killed by the National Guard during an antiwar demonstration.

The 26th Amendment, allowing 18–20 year olds to vote, is ratified.

The Watergate scandal begins with a break-in at the Democratic National Committee headquarters.

Eleven Israeli athletes are killed by terrorists at the Olympic Games in Munich.

The United States pulls out of Vietnam.

Patty Hearst is kidnapped by the Symbionese Liberation Army.

President Nixon resigns.

President Ford pardons Nixon.

South Vietnam falls; North and South Vietnam reunite.

President Carter pardons Vietnam draft evaders.

The U.S. Senate votes to turn Panama Canal over to Panama by the year 2000.

A partial meltdown occurs at the Three Mile Island nuclear plant.

Hostages are taken at the U.S. Embassy in Tehran, Iran.

KEYWORDS

60 Minutes	the Bee Gees
A Chorus Line	bicentennial celebrations
acid rain	Bobby Fischer
Agent Orange	"Bridge Over Troubled Water"
Al Pacino	Camp David peace accords
Ali MacGraw	*Charlie's Angels*
All in the Family	the Chicago Seven trial
Barry Manilow	compact cars

"Copacabana"
Daniel Ellsberg
DDT is banned
Deep Throat
Diana Ross
disco
Doobie Brothers
E.R.A.
the Eagles
Elton John
G.I. Joe toys
gas shortage
The Godfather
Grease
Hank Aaron
Henry Kissinger
I'm OK—You're OK
inflation
James Taylor
Janis Joplin
Jaws
Jesus Christ Superstar
Jimmy Hoffa disappears
John Denver
Jonestown
Laverne and Shirley
Legionnaires' disease
leisure suits
"Love it or leave it"
Love Story
M.A.S.H.
"Make love not war"

Mary Tyler Moore Show
mood rings
Moonies
Muhammad Ali
Nadia Comăneci
Nixon's tapes
OPEC
Pentagon Papers
Robert Redford
Rocky
Roe v. Wade
Saturday Night Fever
the "Saturday Night Massacre"
the Sears Tower is constructed
Sesame Street
shag carpet
"Son of Sam"
Spiro Agnew
Star Wars
Susan B. Anthony dollars
test-tube babies
The Thorn Birds
"Tie a Yellow Ribbon Round
   the Ole Oak Tree"
tie-dye
TV bans cigarette ads
Watergate
Woodward and Bernstein
Woody Allen
Wounded Knee
"You Light Up My Life"

THE 1980s

Presidents of this decade:
- ➥ Ronald Reagan (1981–1989)
- ➥ George H. W. Bush (1989–1993)

John Lennon is killed.

The U.S. hostages are released in the Iranian hostage crisis.

President Ronald Reagan is shot and wounded.

Prince Charles and Lady Diana are wed.

Sandra Day O'Connor becomes the first woman on the U.S. Supreme Court.

Mount St. Helens erupts.

Sally Ride becomes the first U.S. woman in space.

U.S. troops invade Grenada.

The Space Shuttle *Challenger* explodes on liftoff.

A major nuclear accident occurs at the Chernobyl power station.

The Iran-Contra affair hearings are held.

The *Exxon Valdez* spills oil off the Alaskan coast.

Chinese students demonstrate in Tiananmen Square in Beijing.

The Berlin Wall falls after 28 years.

U.S. troops invade Panama.

KEYWORDS

The Accidental Tourist	Cabbage Patch Kids
AIDS	CDs
Amadeus	*Cheers*
arms control talks	*The Cosby Show*
Ayatollah Khomeini	CNN
Beirut	cocaine culture
the Bell System is broken up	Dan Quayle
"Born in the USA"	defense spending
Boy George	*Dynasty*
break dancing	Eddie Murphy

E. T. ("Phone home!")
fear of nuclear war
Gary Hart
Geraldine Ferraro
Ghostbusters
Hands Across America
Hill Street Blues
Imelda Marcos
Indiana Jones
jazzercise
Jim Bakker
John Hinckley
junk bonds
leg warmers
Libya
Little Shop of Horrors
The Love Boat
Madonna
Margaret Thatcher
Mary Lou Retton
Michael Jackson
Mikhail Gorbachev
MTV
Muammar Gaddafi
neon colors
New Coke

Oliver North
the Olympics are held
   in Los Angeles
Pan Am Flight 747
The Phantom of the Opera
the PLO
the preppy look
"Read my lips"
Reaganomics
Rubik's Cubes
Salman Rushdie
"Star Wars" antimissile defense
supply-side economics
televangelists
terrorists
Thirtysomething
Thriller
Tom Cruise
VCRs
velcro
the Vietnam Veterans
   Memorial is constructed
"We Are the World"
"Where's the beef?"
"Who shot J. R.?"
yuppies

THE 1990s

> **Presidents of this decade:**
> - ➤ George H. W. Bush (1989–1993)
> - ➤ William "Bill" Clinton (1993–2001)

Nelson Mandela is freed in South Africa after 27 years in prison.

The U.N. forces fight in the Persian Gulf War.

Professor Anita Hill accuses Judge Clarence Thomas of sexual harassment.

Riots break out in Los Angeles after the acquittal of police officers accused of beating Rodney King.

The World Trade Center is bombed.

The Branch Davidian cult is raided in Waco, TX.

O. J. Simpson is put on trial for murder.

Israeli Prime Minister Yitzhak Rabin is assassinated.

The Alfred P. Murrah Federal Building in Oklahoma City is bombed.

Bombing disrupts the Summer Olympic Games in Atlanta, GA.

Princess Diana is killed in a car accident in Paris.

KEYWORDS

Air Jordans

Alan Greenspan

Anita Hill

balanced budgets

baseball strikes—no
  World Series

Bill Gates

biological weapons

the Bosnian War

bottled water

cellular phones

the Christian Coalition

cloned sheep

Colin Powell

conspiracy theories

the Contract with America

cyberspace

David Koresh

Dilbert

Dr. Kevorkian

Dr. Laura Schlessinger

Dr. Martens shoes

e-mail

ER

El Niño

Ellen DeGeneres

fat-free food
The Fresh Prince of Bel-Air
the Gap
gay rights
global warming
government shutdown
grunge
gun control
the Heaven's Gate cult
the Home Shopping Network
high-pollution days
the Internet
Janet Reno
Kerri Strug
Kurt Cobain
laptops
"Macarena"
Madeleine Albright
Magic Johnson
militia groups
the Million Man March
the *Mir* space station
NAFTA
Nancy Kerrigan
the ozone hole
Paula Jones
Prozac

Pulp Fiction
road rage
Rogaine
Ross Perot
Rush Limbaugh
Saddam Hussein
Seinfeld
The Simpsons
"Stormin' Norman" (General
   Herbert Norman
   Schwarzkopf)
Snapple
sport utility vehicles (SUVs)
Starbucks
talk shows
telecommuting
Tickle Me Elmo
Tiger Woods
Timothy McVeigh
tobacco company lawsuits
TWA Flight 800
the Unabomber
ValuJet
virtual pets
welfare reform
Whitewater

THE 2000s

Presidents of this decade:
- ➡ George W. Bush (2001–2008)
- ➡ Barack Obama (2008–)

The Y2K scare grips the nation.

Terrorists fly hijacked planes into the World Trade Center in New York City and the Pentagon.

The United States begins the "War on Terror" against al-Qaeda.

The euro becomes the sole legal tender for many of the European Union member states.

The Queen Mother dies.

The Space Shuttle *Columbia* explodes.

U.S. and U.K. forces invade Iraq, citing the threat of weapons of mass destruction.

Pope John Paul II dies.

Former Iraq President Saddam Hussein is captured, tried, and executed.

Hurricane Katrina hits New Orleans and the surrounding Gulf States.

A severe economic recession as a result of the 2008 global financial crisis occurs.

Michael Jackson dies.

The first African American President is elected into office.

KEYWORDS

the Abu Ghraib prison scandal
al-Qaeda
American Idol
Arnold Schwarzenegger ("The Governator")
Bernie Madoff
Blackberry phones

BRIC countries
Britney Spears
Chelsey Burnett "Sully" Sullenberger, III, and US Airways Flight 1549
Crocs
The Da Vinci Code

Desperate Housewives
digital cameras
Enron
Facebook
Finding Nemo
global warming
"Gitmo" (Guantánamo Bay)
Google
Hamas
Harry Potter
the Human Genome Project
immigration issues
the iPod
"mad cow disease"
Martha Stewart
the Mexican Drug War
No Child Left Behind

obesity
Osama bin Laden
outsourcing
Pluto stops being a planet
same-sex marriage
SARS
Sex and the City
The Sopranos
stem cell research
sports steroids scandals
the Taliban
texting
the Tea Party movement
Tiger Woods
Twitter/"tweets"
weapons of mass destruction
YouTube

2010–

> **Presidents of this decade:**
> ➥ Barack Obama (2008–)

An earthquake in Haiti kills more than 300,000 people.

The Patient Protection Affordable Care Act is passed into law.

An oil platform explosion in the Gulf of Mexico leads to the largest accidental marine oil spill in history.

An earthquake and tsunami strike Japan, causing the Fukushima Daiichi nuclear crisis.

Osama bin Laden is killed in a raid by U. S. Navy SEALs.

Greece, Spain, and other European countries implement austerity measures in efforts to wind-down the European sovereign-debt crisis.

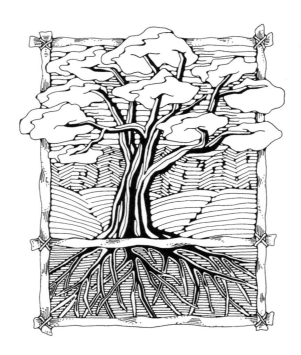

About the Author

Mary Borg is the creator and developer of popular autobiography-writing classes for senior adults. For more than 24 years, she has helped hundreds of men and women write their autobiographies through adult education classes in the northern Colorado area. She is also a full-time history professor at the University of Northern Colorado, teaching American History and Colorado History courses and mentoring secondary social studies student teachers.

Mary Borg would love to help anyone start a Writing Your Life class! You can contact her at mary.borg@unco.edu.